Caroline Wells Healey Dall, Marie E Zakrzewska

A Practical Illustration of Women's Right to Labor

Caroline Wells Healey Dall, Marie E Zakrzewska

A Practical Illustration of Women's Right to Labor

ISBN/EAN: 9783337175290

Printed in Europe, USA, Canada, Australia, Japan

Cover: Foto ©Suzi / pixelio.de

More available books at **www.hansebooks.com**

Lately Published,

(Pages xv. and 184, 16mo; Paper, 50 cts.; Cloth, 63 cents,)

𝕎oman's ℝight to 𝕃abor;

OR,

LOW WAGES AND HARD WORK.

THREE LECTURES BY MRS. C. H. DALL.

I. DEATH OR DISHONOR. | II. VERIFY YOUR CREDENTIALS. III. THE OPENING OF THE GATES.

The spirit and design of these lectures are excellent. — *London Athenæum.*

It is crammed with facts. Mrs. Dall has done in this book what has not been done before, and what was wanted. For this reason, it is a book to be bought, kept, referred to, and lent. — *Christian Examiner.*

Mrs. Dall's explicitness, directness, and earnestness in so worthy a cause, claim our hearty commendation. — *North-American Review.*

The author tells her sad tale with rare refinement, and dignity of speech; with rare force and clearness also; and with so earnest and pure a purpose, that we feel its moral pressed upon us with resistless force. — *Unitarian Monthly.*

Literary culture, patient industry, and an earnest spirit, have been brought to the preparation of this slight volume. The author has written because she feels; and she has written sensibly, gracefully, to the time, and to the point. — *Christian Review.*

She brings her unequalled powers, not to the composition of essays which would not be tolerated from a man, but to the laborious collection of facts, to faithful induction of principles, and to clear and brave admonition. In the quality of her work she stands pre-eminent. — *Chicago Tribune.*

We hope this book will be read by every family in the land. — *New-York Christian Enquirer.*

Her suggestions are enforced by a variety of interesting historical and statistical facts. — *New-York Tribune.*

The subject so ably and earnestly discussed by Mrs. Dall is one of the most important, and, at the same time, one of the most difficult of treatment. — *Dedham Gazette.*

Her views are illustrated and supported by an array of facts which will surprise those who have not looked into the subject. — *Worcester Spy.*

The evidences of a kind heart, close observation, faithful labor, and clear, strong, reasoning faculties, are visible in this little book. — *Montreal Pilot.*

We envy not the moral characteristics of the man whose heart this little work does not set throbbing with sympathy. — *Antislavery Standard.*

The spirit of this little book is so candid, its tone so earnest, and it is so interesting with curious facts and comparisons, that it challenges the attention of all thoughtful men and women. — *G. W. Curtis, in Harpers' Weekly.*

PUBLISHED BY WALKER, WISE, & CO.,

245, WASHINGTON STREET, BOSTON.

𝔓ractical 𝔍llustration

OF

"WOMAN'S RIGHT TO LABOR;"

OR,

A LETTER FROM MARIE E. ZAKRZEWSKA, M.D.

LATE OF BERLIN, PRUSSIA.

EDITED BY

CAROLINE H. DALL,

AUTHOR OF "WOMAN'S RIGHT TO LABOR," "HISTORICAL PICTURES
RETOUCHED," &C. &C.

―――――

" Whoso cures the plague,
Though twice a woman, shall be called a leech."
" And witness: she who did this thing was born
To do it; claims her license in her work."
AURORA LEIGH.

―――――

BOSTON:

WALKER, WISE, AND COMPANY,
245, WASHINGTON STREET.
1860.

"The men (who are prating, too, on their side) cry,
'A woman's function plainly is . . . to talk.'"

"What
He doubts is, whether we can *do* the thing
With decent grace we've not yet done at all.
Now do it."

"Bring your statue:
You have room."

"None of us is mad enough to say
We'll have a grove of oaks upon that slope,
And sink the need of acorns."

PREFACE.

It is due to myself to say, that the manner in which the Autobiography is subordinated to the general subject in the present volume, and also the manner in which it is *veiled* by the title, are concessions to the modesty of her who had the best right to decide in what fashion I should profit by her goodness, and are very far from being my own choice.

CAROLINE H. DALL.

49. BRADFORD STREET, BOSTON,
    Oct. 30, 1860.

𝔄 𝔓𝔯𝔞𝔠𝔱𝔦𝔠𝔞𝔩 𝔉𝔩𝔩𝔲𝔰𝔱𝔯𝔞𝔱𝔦𝔬𝔫

OF

"WOMAN'S RIGHT TO LABOR."

———

IT never happens that a true and forcible word is spoken for women, that, however faithless and unbelieving women themselves may be, some noble men do not with heart and hand attempt to give it efficiency.

If women themselves are hard upon their own sex, men are never so in earnest. They realize more profoundly than women the depth of affection and self-denial in the womanly soul; and they feel also, with crushing certainty, the real significance of the obstacles they have themselves placed in woman's way.

Reflecting men are at this moment ready to help women to enter wider fields of labor, because, on the one side, the destitution and vice they have helped to create appalls their consciousness; and,

1

on the other, a profane inanity stands a perpetual blasphemy in the face of the Most High.

I do not exaggerate. Every helpless woman is such a blasphemy. So, indeed, is every helpless man, where helplessness is not born of idiocy or calamity; but society neither expects, provides for, nor defends, helpless men.

So it happened, that, after the publication of "Woman's Right to Labor," generous men came forward to help me carry out my plans. The best printer in Boston said, "I am willing to take women into my office at once, if you can find women who will submit to an apprenticeship like men." On the same conditions, a distinguished chemist offered to take a class of women, and train them to be first-class apothecaries or scientific observers, as they might choose. To these offers there were no satisfactory responses. "Yes," said the would-be printers, "we will go into an office for six months; but, by that time, our oldest sisters will be married, and our mothers will want us at home."

"An apprenticeship of six years!" exclaimed the young lady of a chemical turn. "I should like to learn very much, so that I could be a chemist, *if I ever had to*; but poison myself for six years over those 'fumes,' not I." It is easy to rail against society and men in general: but it is very painful for a woman to confess her heaviest obstacle to success ; namely, the *weakness of women*. The slave who dances, unconscious of degradation, on the auction-block, is at once the greatest stimulus and the bitterest discouragement of the antislavery reformer : so women, contented in ignominious dependence, restless even to insanity from the need of healthy employment and the perversion of their instincts, and confessedly looking to marriage for salvation, are at once a stimulus to exertion, and an obstacle in our way. But no kind, wise heart will heed this obstacle. Having spoken plain to society, having won the sympathy of men, let us see if we cannot compel the attention of these well-disposed but thoughtless damsels.

" Six years out of the very bloom of our lives to be spent in the printing-office or the laboratory ! " exclaim the dismayed band; and they flutter out of reach along the sidewalks of Beacon Street, or through the mazes of the " Lancers."

But what happens ten years afterward, when, from twenty - six to thirty, they find themselves pushed off the *pavé*, or left to blossom on the wall? Desolate, because father and brother have died;

disappointed, because well-founded hopes of a home or a "career" have failed; impoverished, because they depended on strength or means that are broken, — what have they now to say to the printing-office or the apothecary's shop? They enter both gladly; with quick woman's wit, learning as much in six months as men would in a year; but grumbling and discontented, that, in competing with men who have spent their whole lives in preparation, they can only be paid at half-wages. What does common sense demand, if not that women should make thorough preparation for trades or professions; and, having taken up a resolution, should abide by all its consequences like men?

Before cases like these my lips are often sealed, and my hands drop paralyzed. Not that they alter God's truth, or make the duty of protest against existing wrong any less incumbent: but they obscure the truth; they needlessly complicate the duty.

Perplexed and anxious, I have often felt that what I needed most was an example to set before young girls, — an example not removed by superiority of station, advantage of education, or unwonted endowment, beyond their grasp and imitation.

There was Florence Nightingale. But her fa-

ther had a title: it was fair to presume that her
opportunities were titled also. All the girls I knew
wished they could have gone to the Crimea; while
I was morally certain, that the first amputation
would have turned them all faint. There was
Dorothea Dix: she had money and time. It was
not strange that she had great success; for she
started, a monomaniac in philanthropy, from the
summit of personal independence. Mrs. John Stuart
Mill: had she ever wanted bread? George Sand:
the woman wasn't respectable. In short, whomso-
ever I named, who had pursued with undeviating
perseverance a worthy career, my young friends
had their objections ready. No one had ever
been so poor, so ill educated, so utterly without
power to help herself, as they; and, provoking as
these objections were, I felt that they had force.
My young friends were not great geniuses: they
were ordinary women, who should enter the ordinary walks of life with the ordinary steadfastness
and devotion of men in the same paths; nothing
more. What I wanted was an example, — not too
stilted to be useful, — a life flowing out of circumstances not dissimilar to their own, but marked by
a steady will, an unswerving purpose. As I looked
back over my own life, and wished I could read

them its lessons,—and I looked back a good way;
for I was very young, when the miserable destitution of a drunkard's wife, whom I assisted, showed
me how comfortable a thing it was to rest at the
mercy of the English common law,—as I looked
back over my long interest in the position of woman,
I felt that my greatest drawback had been the want
of such an example. Every practical experiment
that the world recorded had been made under such
peculiar circumstances, or from such a fortuitous
height, that it was at once rejected as a lesson.

One thing I felt profoundly: as men sow they
must reap; and so must women. The practical
misery of the world — its terrible impurity will
never be abated till women prepare themselves
from their earliest years to enter the arena of
which they are ambitious, and stand there at last
mature and calm, but, above all, *thoroughly trained;*
trained also at *the side of the men,* with whom
they must ultimately work; and not likely, therefore, to lose balance or fitness by being thrown, at
the last moment, into unaccustomed relations. A
great deal of nonsense has been talked lately about
the unwillingness of women to enter the reading-
room of the Cooper Institute, where men also
resort.

"A woman's library," in any city, is one of the partial measures that I deprecate: so I only partially rejoice over the late establishment of such a library in New York. I look upon it as one of those half-measures which must be endured in the progress of any desired reform; and, while I wish the Cooper Institute and its reading-room Godspeed with every fibre of my consciousness, I have no words with which to express my shame at the mingled hypocrisy and indelicacy of those who object to use it. What woman stays at home from a ball because she will meet men there? What woman refuses to walk Broadway in the presence of the stronger sex? What woman refuses to buy every article of her apparel from the hands of a man, or to let the woman's tailor or shoemaker take the measure of her waist or foot; try on and approve her coiffure or bernouse?

What are we to think, then, of the delicacy which shrinks from the reading-room frequented by men; which discovers so suddenly that magazines are more embarrassing than mazourkas; that to read in a cloak and hat before a man is more indelicate than to waltz in his presence half denuded by fashion?

Of course, we are to have no patience with it,

and to refuse utterly to entertain a remonstrance so beneath propriety.

The object of my whole life has been to inspire in women a desire for *thorough training* to some special end, and a willingness to share the training of men both for specific and moral reasons. Only by sharing such training can women be sure that they will be well trained ; only by God-ordained, natural communion of all men and women can the highest moral results be reached.

"Free labor and free society:" I have said often to myself, in these two phrases lies hidden the future purification of society. When men and women go everywhere together, the sights they dare not see together will no longer exist.

Fair and serene will rise before them all heights of possible attainment ; and, looking off over the valleys of human endeavor together, they will clear the forest, drain the morass, and improve the interval, stirred by a common impulse.

When neither has any thing to hide from the other, no social duty will seem too difficult to be undertaken ; and, when the interest of each sex is to secure the purity of the other, neither religion nor humanity need despair of the result.

It was while fully absorbed in thoughts and

purposes like these, that, in the autumn of 1856, I
first saw Marie Zakrzewska.* During a short visit
to Boston (for she was then resident in New York),
a friend brought her before a physiological institute,
and she addressed its members.

She spoke to them of her experience in the hospital at Berlin, and showed that the most sinning,
suffering woman never passed beyond the reach of
a woman's sympathy and help. She had not, at
that time, thoroughly mastered the English language; though it was quite evident that she was
fluent, even to eloquence, in German. Now and
then, a word failed her; and, with a sort of indignant contempt at the emergency, she forced unaccustomed words to do her service, with an adroit-
ness and determination that I never saw equalled.
I got from it a new revelation of the power of the
English language. She illustrated her noble and
nervous thoughts with incidents from her own experience, one of which was told in a manner which
impressed it for ever on my consciousness.

" Soon after I entered the hospital," said Marie,
" the nurse called me to a ward where sixteen of
the most forlorn objects had begun to fight with

---

* Pronounced Zak-shef-ska.

each other. The inspector and the young physicians had been called to them, but dared not enter the *mêlée*. When I arrived, pillows, chairs, footstools, and vessels had deserted their usual places; and one stout little woman, with rolling eyes and tangled hair, lifted a vessel of slops, which she threatened to throw all over me, as she exclaimed, 'Don't dare to come here, you green young thing!'

"I went quietly towards her, saying gently, 'Be ashamed, my dear woman, of your fury.'

"Her hands dropped. Seizing me by the shoulder, she exclaimed, 'You don't mean that you look on me as a woman?'

"'How else?' I answered; while she retreated to her bed, all the rest standing in the attitudes into which passion had thrown them.

"'Arrange your beds,' I said; 'and in fifteen minutes let me return, and find every thing right.' When I returned, all was as I had desired; every woman standing at her bedside. The short woman was missing; but, bending on each a friendly glance, I passed through the ward, which never gave me any more trouble.

"When, late at night, I entered my room, it was fragrant with violets. A green wreath surrounded an old Bible, and a little bouquet rested upon it. I did not pause to speculate over this sentimentality, but threw myself weary upon the bed; when a light tap at the door startled me. The short woman entered; and humbling herself on the floor, since she would not sit in my presence, entreated to be heard.

"'You called me a woman,' she said, 'and you pity us. Others call us by the name the world gives us. You would help us, if help were possible. All the girls love you, and are ashamed before you; and therefore *I* hate you — no : I will not hate you any longer. There was a time when I might have been saved, — I and Joanna and Margaret and Louise. We were not bad. Listen to me. If *you* say there is any hope, I will yet be an honest woman.'

"She had had respectable parents ; and, when twenty years old, was deserted by her lover, who left her three months pregnant. Otherwise kind, her family perpetually reproached her with her disgrace, and threatened to send her away. At last, she fled to Berlin; keeping herself from utter starvation, by needlework. In the hospital to which she went for confinement, she took the small-pox. When she came out, with her baby in her arms, her face was covered with red blotches. Not even

the lowest refuge was open to her, her appearance
was so frightful. With her baby dragging at her
empty breast, she wandered through the streets.
An old hag took pity on both; and, carefully
nursed till health returned, her good humor and
native wit made those about her forget her ugly
face. She was in a brothel, where she soon took
the lead. Her child died, and she once more
attempted to earn her living as a seamstress. She
was saved from starvation only by her employer,
who received her as his mistress. Now her
luck changed : she suffered all a woman could;
handled poison and the firebrand. ' I thought of
stealing,' she said, ' only as an amusement: it was
not exciting enough for a trade.' She found herself in prison; and was amused to be punished for
a trifle, when nobody suspected her crime. It was
horrible to listen to these details; more horrible
to witness her first repentance.

"When I thanked her for her violets, she kissed
my hands, and promised to be good.

"While she remained in the hospital, I took her
as my servant, and trusted every thing to her;
and, when finally discharged, she went out to service. She wished to come with me to America.
I could not bring her; but she followed, and,

when I was in Cleveland, inquired for me in New York."

It will be impossible, for those who have not heard such stories from the lips and in the dens of the sufferers, to feel as I felt when this dropped from the pure lips of the lecturer. For the first time I saw a woman who knew what I knew, felt what I felt, and was strong in purpose and power to accomplish our common aim, — the uplifting of the fallen, the employment of the idle, and the purification of society.

I needed no farther introduction to Marie Zakrzewska. I knew nothing of her previous history or condition; but when I looked upon her clear, broad forehead, I saw "Faithful unto death" bound across it like a phylactery. I did not know how many years she had studied; but I saw thoroughness ingrained into her very muscle. I asked no questions of the clear, strong gaze that pierced the assembly; but I felt very sure that it could be as tender as it was keen. For the first time I saw a woman in a public position, about whom I felt thoroughly at ease; competent to all she had undertaken, and who had undertaken nothing whose full relations to her sex and society she did not understand.

I thanked God for the sight, and very little thought that I should see her again. She came once more, and we helped her to establish the Women's Infirmary in New York; again, and we installed her as Resident Physician in the New-England Female Medical College.

I had never felt any special interest in this college. I was willing it should exist as one of the half-way measures of which I have spoken, — like the reading-room in New York; but I was bent on opening the colleges which already existed to women, and I left it to others to nurse the young life of this. The first medical men, I felt assured, would never, in the present state of public opinion, take an interest in a *female* college; and I desired, above all things, to protect women from second-rate instruction.

But, when Marie Zakrzewska took up her residence in Springfield Street, it was impossible to feel indifferent. Here was a woman born to inspire faith; meeting all men as her equals till they proved themselves superior; capable of spreading a contagious fondness for the study of medicine, as Dr. Black once kindled a chemical enthusiasm in Edinburgh.

Often did I ponder her past life, which had left

significant lines on face and form. We met seldom,
— always with perfect trust. Whatever I might
have to say, I should have felt sure of being
understood, if I had not seen her for six months;
nor could she have failed to find a welcome in my
heart for any words of hers.

Then I heard the course of lectures which she
delivered to ladies in the spring of 1860. For the
first time, I heard a woman speak of scientific subjects in a way that satisfied me; nor should I have
blushed to find scientific men among her audience.
I had felt, from the first, that her life might
do what my words never could: namely, inspire
women with faith to try their own experiments;
give them a dignity, which should refuse to look
forward to marriage as an end, while it would
lead them to accept it gladly as a providential help.
I did not fear that she would be untrue to her
vocation, or easily forsake it for a more domestic
sphere. She had not entered it, I could see, without
measuring her own purpose and its use.

It was with such feelings, and such knowledge
of Marie, that in a private conversation, last summer, with Miss Mary L. Booth of New York, I
heard with undisguised pleasure that she had in
her possession an autobiography of her friend, in

the form of a letter. I really longed to get possession of that letter so intensely, that I dared not ask to see it: but I urged Miss Booth to get consent to its publication; "for," I said, "no single thing will help my work, I am convinced, so much."

"I look forward to its publication," she replied, "with great delight: it will be the sole labor of love, of my literary life. But neither you nor I believe in reputations which death and posterity have not confirmed. What reasons could I urge to Marie for its present publication?"

"The good of her own sex," I replied, "and a better knowledge of the intimate relations existing between free labor and a pure society. I know nothing of our friend's early circumstances; but I cannot be mistaken in the imprint they have left. This is one of those rare cases, in which a life may belong to the public before it has closed."

I returned to Boston. Later in the season, Miss Booth visited Dr. Zakrzewska. Imagine my surprise when she came to me one day, and laid before me the coveted manuscript. "It is yours," she said, "to publish if you choose. I have got Marie's consent. She gave it very reluctantly; but her convictions accord with yours, and she does not think she has any right to refuse. As for me," Miss Booth continued, " I resign without regret my dearest literary privilege, because I feel that the position you have earned in reference to ' woman's labor' entitles you to edit it."

In an interview which I afterwards held with Marie Zakrzewska, she gave me to understand, that, had she been of American birth, she would never have consented to the publication of her letter in her lifetime. "But," she said, "I am a foreigner. You who meet me and sustain me are entitled to know something of my previous history. Those whom I most loved are dead; not a word of the record can pain them; not a word but may help some life just now beginning. It will make a good sequel to ' Woman's Right to Labor.' "

" Only too good," I thought. " May God bless the lesson ! "

It was agreed between Miss Booth and myself, that the autobiography should keep its original, simple form, to indicate how and why it was written: so I invite my friends to read it at once with me. Here is something as entertaining as a novel, and as useful as a treatise. Here is a story which must enchant the conservative, while it inspires the reformer. The somewhat hazy forms of Drs. Schmidt and Müller, the king's order to

2

the rebellious electors, the historic prestige of a Prussian locality, — all these will lend a magic charm to the plain lesson which New York and Boston need.

———

NEW YORK, September, 1857.

DEAR MARY,

It is especially for your benefit that I write these facts of my life. I am not a great personage, either through inherited qualifications or the work that I have to show to the world; yet you may find, in reading this little sketch, that with few talents, and very moderate means for developing them, I have accomplished more than many women of genius and education would have done in my place, for the reason that confidence and faith in their own powers were wanting. And, for this reason, I know that this story might be of use to others, by encouraging those who timidly shrink from the field of action, though endowed with all that is necessary to enable them to come forth and do their part in life. The fact that a woman of no extraordinary powers can make her way by the simple determination, that whatever she can do she will do, must inspire those who are fitted to do much, yet who do nothing because they are not accustomed to determine and decide for themselves.

I do not intend to weary you with details of my childhood, as I think that children are generally very uninteresting subjects of conversation to any except their parents, who naturally discover what is beautiful and attractive in them, and appreciate what is said in correspondence with their own feelings. I shall, therefore, only tell you a few facts of this period of my life, which I think absolutely necessary to illustrate my character and nature.

I was born in Berlin, Prussia, on the 6th of September, 1829 ; and am the eldest of a family of five sisters and one brother. My early childhood passed happily, though heavy clouds of sorrow and care at times overshadowed our family circle. I was of a cheerful disposition ; and was always in good humor, even when sick. I was quiet and gentle in all my amusements : my chief delight consisting in telling stories to my sister, one year younger than myself, who was always glad to listen to these products of my imagination, which were wholly original ; for no stories were told me, nor had I any children's books. My heroes and heroines were generally distinguished for some

mental peculiarity, — being kind or cruel, active
or indolent, — which led them into all sorts of ad-
ventures till it suited my caprice to terminate their
career. In all our little affairs, I took the lead,
planning and directing every thing; while my
playmates seemed to take it for granted, that it
was their duty to carry out my commands.

My memory is remarkable in respect to events
that occurred at this time, while it always fails to
recall dates and names. When twenty years of age,
I asked my father what sort of a festival he took me
to once, in company with a friend of his with only
one arm, when we walked through meadows where
daisies were blossoming in millions, and where we
rode in carriages that went round continually until
they were wound up. My father answered, with
much surprise, that it was a public festival of
the cabinet-makers, which was celebrated in a
neighboring village; and that I was, at that time,
only nineteen months old.

He was so much interested in my story, that
I related another of my memories. One dark
morning, my mother wakened me, and hastened
my dressing. After this was accomplished, she
handed me a cup of something which I had never
tasted before, and which was as disagreeable as

assafœtida in later years. This was some coffee, which I had to take instead of my usual milk. Then I went with my father to the large park called Thiergarten, where we saw the sun rise. I began to spring about; looking at the big oaks which seemed to reach into the heavens, or stooping down to pluck a flower. Birds of all kinds were singing in chorus, while the flower-beds surrounding the statue of Flora scented the pure morning air with the sweetest of perfumes. The sun ascended, meanwhile, from the edge of a little pond covered with water-lilies. I was intoxicated with joy. The feeling of that morning is as fresh to-day as when I related this to my father. I know I walked till I got fairly tired, and we reached a solitary house beyond the park. Probably fatigue took entire possession of me; for I remember nothing more till we were on our way home, and the sun was setting. Then I begged for some large yellow plums which I saw in the stores. My father bought some, but gave me only a few; while I had a desire for all, and stole them secretly from his pockets; so that, when we reached home, I had eaten them all. I was sick after I went to bed, and remember taking some horrible stuff the next morning (probably rhubarb); thus ending the day, which had opened so poetically, in rather a prosaic manner. When I repeated this, my parents laughed, and said that I was only twenty-six months old, when my father's pride in his oldest child induced him to take me on this visit; when I walked the whole way, which was about *nine miles*. These anecdotes are worth preserving, only because they indicate an impressionable nature, and great persistence of muscular endurance. It is peculiar, that between these two events, and a third which occurred a year after, every thing should be a blank.

A little brother was then born to me, and lay undressed upon a cushion, while my father cried with sobs. I had just completed my third year, and could not understand why, the next day, this little thing was carried off in a black box.

From that time, I remember almost every day's life.

I very soon began to manifest the course of my natural tendencies. Like most little girls, I was well provided with dolls; and, on the day after a new one came into my possession, I generally discovered that the dear little thing was ill, and needed to be nursed and doctored. Porridges and teas were accordingly cooked on my little toy stove, and administered to the poor doll, until the *papier-maché* was thoroughly saturated and broken; when she was considered dead, and preparations were made for her burial, — this ceremony being repeated over and over again. White dresses were put on for the funeral; a cricket was turned upside-down to serve as the coffin; my mother's flower-pots furnished the green leaves for decoration; and I delivered the funeral oration in praise of the little sufferer, while placing her in the tomb improvised of chairs. I hardly ever joined the other children in their plays, except upon occasions like these, when I appeared in the characters of doctor, priest, and undertaker; generally improving the opportunity to moralize; informing my audience, that Ann (the doll) had died in consequence of disobeying her mother by going out before she had recovered from the measles, &c. Once I remember moving my audience to tears by telling them that little Ann had been killed by her brother, who, in amusing himself with picking off the dry skin after she had had the scarlatina, had carelessly, torn off the real skin over the heart, as they could see; thus leaving it to beat in the air, and causing the little one to die. This happened after we had all had the scarlatina.

When five years old, I was sent to a primary school. Here I became the favorite of the teacher of arithmetic; for which study I had quite a fancy. The rest of the teachers disliked me. They called me unruly because I would not obey arbitrary demands without receiving some reason, and obstinate because I insisted on following my own will when I knew that I was in the right. I was told that I was not worthy to be with my playmates; and when I reached the highest class in the school, in which alone the boys and girls were taught separately, I was separated from the latter, and was placed with the boys by way of punishment, receiving instructions with them from men, while the girls in the other class were taught by women. Here I found many friends. I joined the boys in all their sports; sliding and snow-balling with them in winter, and running and playing ball in summer. With them I was merry, frank, and self-possessed; while with the girls I was quiet, shy, and awkward. I never made friends with the girls, or felt like approaching them.

Once only, when I was eleven years old, a girl in the young ladies' seminary in which I had been placed when eight years of age won my affection. This was Elizabeth Hohenhorst, a child of twelve, remarkably quiet, and disposed to melancholy. She was a devout Catholic; and, knowing that she was fated to become a nun, was fitting herself for that dreary destiny, which rendered her very sentimental. She was full of fanciful visions, but extremely sweet and gentle in her manners. My love for her was unbounded. I went to church in her company, was present at all the religious festivals, and accompanied her to receive religious instruction: in short, I made up my mind to become a Catholic, and, if possible, a nun like herself. My parents, who were Rationalists, belonging to no church, gave me full scope to follow out my own inclinations; leaving it to my nature to choose for me a fitting path. This lasted until Elizabeth went for the first time to the confessional; and, when the poor innocent child could find no other sin of which to speak than the friendship which she cherished for a Protestant, the priest forbade her to continue this, until I, too, had become a Catholic; reminding her of the holiness of her future career. The poor girl conscientiously promised to obey. When I came the next morning and spoke to her as usual, she turned away from me, and burst into tears. Surprised and anxious, I asked what was the matter; when, in a voice broken with sobs, she told me the whole story, and begged me to become a Catholic as soon as I was fourteen years old. Never in my whole life shall I forget that morning. For a moment, I gazed on her with the deepest emotion, pitying her almost more than myself; then suddenly turned coldly and calmly away, without answering a single word. My mind had awakened to the despotism of Roman Catholicism, and the church had lost its expected convert. I never went near her again, and never exchanged another word with her. This was the only friend I had during eight and a half years of uninterrupted attendance at school.

A visit that I paid to my maternal grandfather, when seven or eight years old, made a strong impression on my mind. My grandfather, on his return from the war of 1813–15, in which he had served, had received from the authorities of Prenzlau (the city in which he lived) a grant of a half-ruined cloister, with about a hundred acres of uncultivated land attached, by way of acknowledgment for his services. He removed thither with his family; and shortly after invited the widows of some soldiers, who lived in the city, to occupy the apartments which he did not need. The habitable rooms were soon filled to overflowing with

widows and orphans, who went to work with him
to cultivate the ground. It was not long before
crippled and invalid soldiers arrived, begging to be
allowed to repair the cloister, and to find a shelter
also within its walls. They were set to work at
making brick, the material for which my grandfather had discovered on his land: and, in about
five years, an institution was built, the more valuable from the fact that none lived there on charity,
but all earned what they needed by cultivating the
ground ; having first built their own dwelling,
which, at this time, looked like a palace, surrounded
by trees, grass, and flowers. Here, in the evening,
the old soldiers sung martial songs, or told stories
of the wars to the orphans gathered about them,
while resting from the labors of the day.

I tell you of this institution so minutely, to prove
to you how wrong it is to provide charitable homes
for the poor as we provide them, — homes in which
the charity always humiliates and degrades the individual. Here you have an instance in which poor
crippled invalids and destitute women and children
established and supported themselves, under the
guidance of a clear-headed, benevolent man, who
said, " Do what you like, but work for what you
need." He succeeded admirably, though he died a

very poor man ; his younger children becoming
inmates of the establishment, until they were adopted by their relatives.

When I visited my grandfather, the " convent,"
as he insisted on calling it, — rejecting any name
that would have indicated a charitable institution, —
contained about a hundred invalid soldiers, a hundred old women, and two hundred and fifty orphans.
One of the wings of the building was fitted up as a
hospital, and a few of the rooms were occupied by
lunatics.   It was my greatest delight to take my
grandfather's hand at noon, as he walked up and
down the dining - room, between the long tables,
around which were grouped so many cheerful,
hearty faces; and I stood before him with an admiration that it is impossible to describe, as he
prayed, with his black velvet cap in his hand, before and after dinner ; though I could not comprehend why he should thank another person for
what had been done, when every one there told
me that all that they had they owed to my grandfather.

One afternoon, on returning from the dining-room
to his study, I spied on his desk a neatly written
manuscript.   I took it up, and began to read.   It
was a dissertation on immortality, attempting by

scientific arguments to prove its impossibility. I became greatly interested, and read on without noticing that my grandfather had left the room, nor that the large bell had rung to call the family to dinner. My grandfather, a very punctual man, who would never allow lingering, came back to call and to reprimand me; when he suddenly started on seeing the paper in my hands, and, snatching it from me, tore it in pieces, exclaiming, "That man is insane, and will make this child so too!" A little frightened, I went to the dinner-table, thinking as much about my grandfather's words as about what I had read; without daring, however, to ask who this man was. The next day, curiosity mastered fear. I asked my grandfather who had written that paper; and was told, in reply, that it was poor crazy Jacob. I then begged to see him; but this my grandfather decidedly refused, saying that he was like a wild beast, and lay, without clothes, upon the straw. I knew nothing of lunatics; and the idea of a wild man stimulated my curiosity to such an extent, that, from that time, I teased my grandfather incessantly to let me see Jacob, until he finally yielded, to be rid of my importunity, and led me to the cell in which he was confined. What a spectacle presented itself in the house that I had looked on as the abode of so much comfort! On a bundle of straw, in a corner of a room, with no furniture save its bare walls, sat a man, clad only in a shirt; with the left hand chained to the wall, and the right foot to the floor. An inkstand stood on the floor by his side; and on his knee was some paper, on which he was writing. His hair and beard were uncombed, and his fine eyes glared with fury as we approached him. He tried to rise, ground his teeth, made grimaces, and shook his fist at my grandfather, who tried in vain to draw me out of the room. But, escaping from his grasp, I stepped towards the lunatic, who grew more quiet when he saw me approach; and I tried to lift the chain, which had attracted my attention. Then, finding it too heavy for me, I turned to my grandfather, and asked, " Does not this hurt the poor man?" I had hardly spoken the words when his fury returned, and he shrieked, —

" Have I not always told you that you were cruel to me? Must this child come to convince you of your barbarity? Yes: you have no heart."

I looked at my grandfather: all my admiration of him was gone; and I said, almost commandingly, —

" Take off these chains! It is bad of you to tie this man!"

The man grew calm at once, and asked imploringly to be set free ; promising to be quiet and tractable if my grandfather would give him a trial. This was promised him : his chains were removed the same day; and Jacob was ever after not only harmless and obedient, but also a very useful man in the house.

I never afterwards accompanied my grandfather. I had discovered a side in his nature which repelled me. I spent the remainder of my visit in the workrooms and the sickroom, always secretly fearing that I should meet with some new cruelty ; but no such instance ever came to my view.

On my return from my grandfather's, I found that a cousin had suddenly become blind. She was soon after sent to the ophthalmic hospital, where she remained for more than a year ; and, during this time, I was her constant companion after school-hours. I was anxious to be useful to her ; and, being gentler than the nurse, she liked to have me wash out the issues that were made in her back and arms. The nurse, who was very willing to be relieved of the duty, allowed me to cleanse the eyes of the girl next my cousin ; and thus these cares were soon made to depend on my daily visit. Child as I was, I could not help observing the

carelessness of the nurses, and their great neglect
of cleanliness. One day, when the head-nurse had
washed the floor, leaving pools of water standing
under the beds, the under-nurse found fault with it,
and said, " I shall tell the doctor, when he comes,
why it is that the patients always have colds."
" Do," said the head-nurse. " What do men understand of such matters? If they knew any thing
about them, they would long ago have taken care
that the mattress upon which one patient dies
should always be changed before another comes
in." This quarrel impressed itself upon my memory; and the wish rose in my mind, that some day
I might be head-nurse, to prevent such wrongs, and
to show kindness to the poor lunatics.

At the end of the year, my cousin left the hospital. At the same time, trouble and constant sickness fell upon our family. My father, who held
liberal opinions and was of an impetuous tempera-
ment, manifested some revolutionary tendencies,
which drew upon him the displeasure of the government, and caused his dismissal, with a very small
pension, from his position as military officer. This
involved us in great pecuniary difficulties; for our
family was large, and my father's income too small
to supply the most necessary wants; while to obtain

other occupation for the time was out of the question. In this emergency, my mother determined to petition the city government for admission to the school of midwives established in Berlin, in order in this manner to aid in the support of the family. Influential friends of my father secured her the election; and she was admitted to the school in 1839, I being at that time ten years of age.

The education of midwives for Berlin requires a two years' course of study, during six months of which they are obliged to reside in the hospital, to receive instructions from the professors together with the male students. My mother went there in the summer of 1840. I went to stay at the house of an aunt, who wished my company; and the rest of the children were put out to board together.

In a few weeks, my eyes became affected with weakness, so that I could neither read nor write; and I begged my mother to let me stay with her in the hospital. She applied for permission to the director, and received a favorable answer. I was placed under the care of one of the physicians (Dr. Müller), who took a great fancy to me, and made me go with him wherever he went while engaged in the hospital. My eyes being bandaged, he led me

by the hand, calling me his "little blind doctor."
In this way I was constantly with him, hearing
all his questions and directions, which impressed
themselves the more strongly on my mind from
the fact that I could not see, but had to gain all
my knowledge through hearing alone.

One afternoon, when I had taken the bandage
off my eyes for the first time, Dr. Müller told me
that there was a corpse of a young man to be seen
in the dead-house, that had turned completely green
in consequence of poison that he had eaten. I went
there after my rounds with him: but finding the
room filled with relatives, who were busily engaged
in adorning the body with flowers, I thought that I
would not disturb them, but would wait until they
had gone before I looked at it; and went meanwhile
through the adjoining rooms. These were all
freshly painted. The dissecting-tables, with the necessary apparatus, stood in the centre; while the
bodies, clad in white gowns, were ranged on boards
along the walls. I examined every thing; came
back, and looked to my heart's content at the poi-
soned young man, without noticing that not only
the relatives had left, but that the prosector had
also gone away, after locking up the whole building. I then went a second time to the other rooms,

and looked again at every thing there; and at last, when it became dark and I could not leave the house, sat down upon the floor, and went to sleep, after knocking for half an hour at the door, in the hope that some passer might hear.

My mother, who knew that I had gone with Dr. Müller, did not trouble herself about me until nine o'clock, when she grew uneasy at my stay; and, thinking that he might have taken me to his rooms, went there in search of me, but found that he was out, and that the doors were locked. She then inquired of the people in the house whether they knew any thing about me, and was told that they had last seen me going into the dead-house. Alarmed at this intelligence, my mother hastened to the prosector, who unwillingly went with her to the park in which the dead-house stood, assuring her all the way that I could not possibly be there; when, on opening the door, he saw me sitting close by, on the floor, fast asleep.

In a few days after this adventure, I recovered the use of my eyes. As it was at this time the summer vacation, in which I had no school-tasks, I asked Dr. Müller for some books to read. He inquired what kind of books I wanted. I told him, "Books about history;" upon which he gave me two huge volumes,—The "History of Midwifery" and the "History of Surgery." Both were so interesting, that I read them through during the six weeks of vacation; which occupied me so closely, that even my friend Dr. Müller could not lay hold of me when he went his morning and evening rounds. From this time I date my study of medicine; for, though I did not continue to read upon the subject, I was instructed in the no less important branch of psychology by a new teacher, whom I found on my return to school at the close of the summer vacation.

To explain better how my mind was prepared for such teaching, I must go back to my position in school. In both schools that I attended, I was praised for my punctuality, industry, and quick perception. Beloved I was in neither: on the contrary, I was made the target for all the impudent jokes of my fellow-pupils; ample material for which was furnished in the carelessness with which my hair and dress were usually arranged; these being left to the charge of a servant, who troubled herself very little about how I looked, provided that I was whole and clean. The truth was, I often presented a ridiculous appearance; and once I could not help laughing heartily at myself, on see-

ing my own face by accident in a glass, with one
braid of hair commencing over the right eye, and
the other over the left ear. I quietly hung a map
over the glass to hide the ludicrous picture, and
continued my studies; and most likely appeared in
the same style the next day. My face, besides, was
neither handsome, nor even prepossessing; a large
nose overshadowing the undeveloped features: and
I was ridiculed for my ugliness, both in school and
at home, where an aunt of mine, who disliked me
exceedingly, always said, in describing plain people,
"Almost as ugly as Marie."

Another cause arose to render my position at
school still more intolerable. In consequence of
the loss of his position in the army, my father
could no longer afford to pay my school-bills; and
was about, in consequence, to remove me from
school; when the principal offered to retain me
without pay, although she disliked me, and did not
hesitate to show it, any more than to tell me, whenever I offended her, that she would never keep so
ugly and naughty a child *without being paid for it*,
were it not for the sake of so noble a father.

These conditions and harsh judgments made me
a philosopher. I heard myself called obstinate
and wilful, only because I believed myself in the

right, and persisted in it. I felt that I was not maliciously disposed towards any one, but wished well to all; and I offered my services not only willingly, but cheerfully, wherever they could be of the least use; and saw them accepted, and even demanded, by those who could not dispense with them, though they shunned and ridiculed me the same as before. I felt that they only sought me when they needed me: this made me shrink still more from their companionship; and, when my sister did not walk home from school with me, I invariably went alone.

The idea that I might not wish to attach myself to playmates of this sort never occurred to any one; but I was constantly reproached with having no friends among my schoolfellows, and was told that no one could love so disagreeable and repelling a child. This was a severe blow to my affectionate nature; but I bore it calmly, consoling myself with the thought that they were wrong, — that they did not understand me, — and that the time would come, when they would learn that a great, warm heart was concealed beneath the so-called repulsive exterior. But, however soothing all this was for the time, a feeling of bitterness grew up within me. I began to be provoked at my ugliness, which I

believed to be excessive. I speculated why parents
so kind and good as mine should be deprived of their
means of support, merely because my father would
not consent to endure wrong and imposition. I
was indignant at being told, that it was only for my
father's sake that I was retained in a school where
I tried to do my best, and where I always won the
highest prizes ; and I could not see why, at home,
I should be forced to do housework when I wanted
to read, while my brother, who wished to work,
was compelled to study. When I complained of
this last grievance, I was told that I was a girl,
and never could learn much, but was only fit to
become a housekeeper. All these things threw me
upon my own resources, and taught me to make
the most of every opportunity, custom and habit
to the contrary notwithstanding.

It was at this juncture that I found, on my return to school, the psychologic instructor of whom
I have spoken, in a newly engaged teacher of
history, geography, and arithmetic ; all of which
were my favorite studies. With this man I formed
a most peculiar friendship : he being twenty years
older than myself, and in every respect a highly
educated man ; I, a child of twelve, neglected in
every thing except in my common-school education.

He began by calling my attention to the carelessness of my dress and the rudeness of my manners, and was the first one who ever spoke kindly to me on the subject. I told him all my thoughts; that I did not mean to be disagreeable, but that every one thought that I could not be otherwise; that I was convinced that I was good enough at heart; and that I had at last resigned myself to my position, as something that could not be helped. My new friend lectured me on the necessity of attracting others by an agreeable exterior and courteous manners; and proved to me that I had unconsciously repelled them by my carelessness, even when trying the most to please. His words made a deep impression on me. I thanked him for every reproach, and strove to do my best to gain his approbation. Henceforth my hair was always carefully combed, my dress nicely arranged, and my collar in its place; and, as I always won the first prizes in the school, two of the other teachers soon grew friendly towards me, and began to manifest their preference quite strongly. In a few months I became a different being. The bitterness that had been growing up within me gradually disappeared; and I began to have confidence in myself, and to try to win the companion-

ship of the other children. But a sudden change
took place in my schoolmates, who grew envious
of the preference shown me by the teachers. Since
they could no longer ridicule me for the carelessness
of my dress, they now began to reproach me for
my vanity, and to call me a coquette, who only
thought of pleasing through appearances. This
blow was altogether too hard for me to bear. I
knew that they were wrong : for, with all the care
I bestowed on my dress, it was not half so fine as
theirs ; as I had but two calico dresses, which I
wore alternately, a week at a time, through the
summer. I was again repelled from them ; and at
noon, when the rest of the scholars went home, I
remained with my teacher-friend in the schoolroom,
assisting him in correcting the exercises of the pupils. I took the opportunity to tell him of the
curious envy that had taken possession of the girls ;
upon which he began to explain to me human nature
and its fallacies, drawing inferences therefrom for
personal application. He found a ready listener
in me. My inclination to abstract thought, com-
bined with the unpleasant experience I had had in
life, made me an attentive pupil, and fitted me to
comprehend his reasoning in the broadest sense.
For fifteen months, I thus spent the noon-hour with

him in the schoolroom; receiving lessons in logic, and reasoning upon concrete and abstract matters, that have since proved of far more psychologic value to me than ten years of reading on the same subjects could do. A strong attachment grew up between us: he became a necessity to me, and I revered him like an oracle. But his health failed; and he left the school at the end of these fifteen months, in a consumption. Shortly after, he sent to the school for me one morning to ask me to visit him on his deathbed. I was not permitted to leave the class until noon; when, just as I was preparing to go, a messenger came to inform the principal that he had died at eleven. This blow fell so heavily upon me, that I wished to leave the school at once. I was forced to stay three weeks longer, until the end of the quarter; when I left the schoolroom on the 1st of April, 1843, at the age of thirteen years and seven months, and never entered it again.

On the same day that I quitted my school, an aunt, with whom I was a favorite, was attacked with a violent hemorrhage from the lungs, and wished me to come to stay with her. This suited my taste. I went; and, for a fortnight, was her sole nurse.

Upon my return home, my father told me, that, having quitted school, I must now become a thorough housekeeper, of whom he might be proud; as this was the only thing for which girls were intended by nature. I cheerfully entered upon my new apprenticeship, and learned how to sweep, to scrub, to wash, and to cook. This work answered very well as long as the novelty lasted; but, as soon as this wore off, it became highly burdensome. Many a forenoon, when I was alone, instead of sweeping and dusting, I passed the hours in reading books from my father's library, until it grew so late, that I was afraid that my mother, who had commenced practice, would come home, and scold me for not attending to my work; when I would hurry to get through, doing every thing so badly, that I had to hear daily that I was good for nothing, and a nuisance in the world; and that it was not at all surprising that I was not liked in school, for nobody could ever like or be satisfied with me.

Meanwhile, my mother's practice gradually increased; and her generous and kindly nature won the confidence of hundreds, who, wretchedly poor, found in her, not only a humane woman, but a most skilful practitioner. The poor are good judges of professional qualifications. Without the aid that

money can buy, without the comforts that the wealthy hardly heed, and without friends whose advice is
prompted by intelligence, they must depend entirely
upon the skill and humanity of those to whom they
apply.   Their life and happiness are placed in the
hands of the physician, and they jealously regard
the one to whom they intrust them.   None but a
good practitioner can gain fame and praise in this
class, which is thought so easily satisfied.   It is
often said, "Oh! those people are poor, and will
be glad of any assistance."   Far from it.   There
is no class so entirely dependent for their subsist-
ence upon their strength and health; these constitute their sole capital, their stock in trade: and,
when sick, they anxiously seek out the best physicians; for, if unskilfully attended, they may lose
their all, their fortune, and their happiness.

My mother went everywhere, both night and day;
and it soon came to pass, that when she was sent for,
and was not at home, I was deputed to go in search
of her.   In this way I gradually became a regular
appendage to my mother; going with her in the
winter nights from place to place, and visiting those
whom she could not visit during the day.   I remember, that in January, 1845, my mother attended
thirty-five women in childbed, — the list of names

is still in my possession,—and visited from sixteen to twenty-five daily, with my assistance. I do not think, that, during the month, we were in bed for one whole night. Two-thirds of these patients were unable to pay a cent. During these years, I learned all of life that it was possible for a human being to learn. I saw nobleness in dens, and meanness in palaces; virtue among prostitutes, and vice among so-called respectable women. I learned to judge human nature correctly; to see goodness where the world found nothing but faults, and also to see faults where the world could see nothing but virtue. The experience thus gained cost me the bloom of youth; yet I would not exchange it for a life of everlasting juvenescence. To keep up appearances is the aim of every one's life; but to fathom these appearances, and judge correctly of what is beneath them, ought to be the aim of those who seek to draw true conclusions from life, or to benefit others by real sympathy.

One fact I learned, both at this time and afterwards; namely, that men always sympathize with fallen and wretched women, while women themselves are the first to raise and cast the stone at them. Why is this? Have not women as much feeling as men? Why, women are said to be made

up entirely of feeling. How does it happen, then,
that women condemn where men pity? Do they
do this in the consciousness of their own superior
virtue? Ah, no! for many of the condemning are
no better than the condemned. The reason is, that
men know the world; that is, they know the obstacles in the path of life, and that they draw lines to
exclude women from earning an honest livelihood,
while they throw opportunities in their way to
earn their bread by shame. All men are aware of
this: therefore the good as well as the bad give
pity to those that claim it. It is my honest and
earnest conviction, that the reason that men are
unwilling for women to enter upon public or business life is, not so much the fear of competition, or
the dread lest women should lose their gentleness,
and thus deprive society of this peculiar charm, as
the fact that they are ashamed of the foulness of
life which exists outside of the house and home.
The good man knows that it is difficult to purify it:
the bad man does not wish to be disturbed in his
prey upon society. If I could but give to all women the tenth part of my experience, they would
see that this is true; and would see, besides, that
only faith in ourselves and in each other is needed
to work a reformation. Let woman enter fully

into business, with its serious responsibilities and duties; let it be made as honorable and as profitable to her as to men; let her have an equal opportunity for earning competence and comfort, — and we shall need no other purification of society. Men are no more depraved than women; or, rather, the total depravity of mankind is a lie.

From the time of my leaving school until I was fifteen years old, my life was passed, as I have described, in doing housework, attending the sick with my mother, and reading a few books of a scientific and literary character. At the end of this time, a letter came from an aunt of my mother's, who was ill, and whose adopted daughter (who was my mother's sister) was also an invalid, requesting me to visit and nurse them. I went there in the fall. This was probably the most decisive event of my life. My great-aunt had a cancer that was to be taken out. The other was suffering from a nervous affection, which rendered her a confirmed invalid. She was a most peculiar woman, and was a clairvoyant and somnambulist of the most decided kind. Though not ill-natured, she was full of caprices that would have exhausted the patience of the most enduring of mortals.

This aunt of mine had been sick in bed for seven

years with a nervous derangement, which baffled the most skilful physicians who had visited her. Her senses were so acute, that one morning she fell into convulsions from the effect of distant music which she heard. None of us could perceive it, and we fully believed that her imagination had produced this result. But she insisted upon it; telling us that the music was like that of the Bohemian miners, who played nothing but polkas. I was determined to ascertain the truth; and really found, that, in a public garden one and a half miles from her house, such a troop had played all the afternoon. No public music was permitted in the city, because the magistrate had forbidden it on her account.

She never was a Spiritualist, though she frequently went into what is now called a trance. She spoke, wrote, sang, and had presentiments of the finest kind, in this condition, — far better than I have ever seen here in America in the case of the most celebrated mediums.

She even prescribed for herself with success, yet was not a Spiritualist. She was a somnambulist; and, though weak enough when awake, threatened several times to pull the house down, by her violence, in this condition. She had strength like a lion, and no man could manage her. I saw the same thing in the hospital later. This aunt is now healthy; not cured by her own prescriptions or the magnetic or infinitesimal doses of Dr. Arthur Lutze, but by a strong emotion which took possession of her at the time of my great-aunt's death. She is not sorry that she has lost all these strange powers, but heartily glad of it. When she afterwards visited us in Berlin, she could speak calmly and quietly of the perversion to which the nervous system may become subject, if managed wrongly; and could not tell how glad she was to be rid of all the emotions and notions she had been compelled to dream out. Over-care and over-anxiety had brought this about; and the same causes could again bring on a condition which the ancients deemed holy, and which the psychologist treats as one bordering on insanity.

The old aunt was extremely suspicious and avaricious. Eight weeks after my arrival, she submitted to an operation. The operating surgeon found me so good an assistant, that he intrusted me often with the succeeding dressing of the wound. For six weeks, I was the sole nurse of the two; going from one room to the other both night and day, and attending to the household matters beside, with no other

assistant than a woman who came every morning
for an hour or two to do the rough work ; while an
uncle and a boy-cousin were continually troubling
me with their torn buttons, &c.

I learned in this time to be cheerful and light-
hearted in all circumstances ; going often into the
anteroom to have a healthy, hearty laugh.   My
surroundings were certainly any thing but inspiring.
I had the sole responsibility of the two sick women ;
the one annoying me with her caprices, the other
with her avarice.   In one room, I heard fanciful
forebodings ; in the other, reproaches for having
used a teaspoonful too much sugar.   I always had
to carry the key of the storeroom to the old aunt,
in order that she might be sure that I could not
go in and eat bread when I chose.   At the end of
six weeks, she died ; and I put on mourning for the
only time in my life, certainly not through grief.

Shortly after the death of my aunt, the attending physician introduced me to a disciple of Hahne-
mann, by the name of Arthur Lutze ; who was, I
think, a doctor of philosophy, — certainly not of
medicine.   Besides being an infinitesimal homœopa-
thist, this man was a devotee to mesmerism.   He
became very friendly towards me, and supplied me
with books ; telling me that I would not only make

a good homœopathic physician, but also an excellent medium for mesmerism, magnetism, &c. At all events, I was glad to get the books, which I read industriously; while he constantly supplied me with new ones, so that I had quite a library when he left the place, which he did before my return He, too, lived in Berlin, and inquired my residence; promising to visit me there, and to teach me the art he practised.

I remained with my aunt until late in the spring; when my health failed, and I returned home. I was very ill for a time with brain-fever; but at last recovered, and set to work industriously to search for information in respect to the human body. Dr. Lutze kept his word: he visited me at my home, gave me more books, and directed my course of reading. But my father, who had become reconciled to my inclination to assist my mother, was opposed to homœopathy, and especially opposed to Dr. Arthur Lutze. He even threatened to turn him out of the house, if I permitted him to visit me again; and burned all my books, except one that I snatched from the flames.

From this time, I was resolved to learn all that I could about the human system. I read all the books on the subject that I could get, and tried

besides to educate myself in other branches. My
father was satisfied with this disposition, and was
glad to hear me propose to have a French teacher in
the house, both for my sake and for that of the other
children. I studied in good earnest by myself; at
the same time, going through the usual discipline
of German girls. I learned plain sewing, dress-
making, and the management of the household; but
was allowed to use my leisure time as I pleased.
When my sisters went skating, I remained at home
to study; when they went to balls and theatres, I
was thought the proper person to stay to watch the
house. Having become so much older, I was now
of great assistance to my mother in her business.
No one complained any longer of my ugliness or
my rudeness. I was always busy; and, when at
liberty, always glad to do what I could for others;
and, though these years were full of hardships,
I consider them among the happiest of my life. I
was as free as it was possible for any German girl
to be.

My household duties, however, continued distaste-
ful to me, much to the annoyance of my father,
who still contended that this was the only sphere of
woman. From being so much with my mother, I
had lost all taste for domestic life : any thing out of

doors was preferable to the monotonous routine of the household. I at length determined to follow my inclinations by studying, in order to fit myself to become a practitioner of midwifery, as is usual in Berlin. My father was satisfied, and pleased with this idea, which opened the way to an independent, respectable livelihood; for he never really wished to have us seek this in marriage. My mother did not like my resolution at all. She practised, not because she liked the profession, but because in this way she obtained the means of being independent, and of aiding in the education of the children. I persisted, however, in my resolution; and immediately took measures to carry it into effect by going directly to Dr. Joseph Hermann Schmidt, the Professor of Midwifery in the University and Schools for Midwives, and Director of the Royal Hospital Charité ; while my father, who for several years held the position of a civil officer, made the application to the city magistrates for me to be admitted as a pupil to the School for Midwives, in which my mother had been educated. In order to show the importance of this step, it is necessary to explain more fully the history and organization of the school.

About 1735, Justina Ditrichin (the wife of Sie-

gemund, a distinguished civil officer of Prussia)
was afflicted with an internal disease which baffled
the skill of the midwives, who had pronounced her
pregnant, and none of whom could define her dis-
order. ' After many months of suffering, she was
visited by the wife of a poor soldier, who told
her what ailed her; in consequence of which, she
was cured by her physicians. This circumstance
awakened in the mind of the lady an intense desire
to study midwifery; which she did, and afterwards
practised it with such success, that, in consequence
of her extensive practice, she was obliged to confine
herself solely to irregular cases. She performed
all kinds of operations with masterly skill, and
wrote the first book on the subject ever published
in Germany by a woman. She was sent for from
all parts of Germany, and was appointed body-
physician of the Queen, and the ladies of the court,
of Prussia and Mark Brandenburg. Through her
influence, schools were established, in which women
were instructed in the science and the art of ob-
stetrics. She also taught many herself; and a very
successful and respectable practice soon grew up
among women. After her death, however, this was
discountenanced by the physicians, who brought it
into such disrepute by their ridicule, that the edu-

cated class of women withdrew from the profession, leaving it in the hands of ignorant pretenders, who continued to practise it until 1818 ; when public attention was called to the subject, and strict laws were enacted, by which women were required to call in a male practitioner in every irregular case of confinement, under penalty of from one to twenty years of imprisonment, and the forfeiture of the right to practise. These laws still continue in force ; and a remarkable case is recorded by Dr. Schmidt of a woman, who, feeling her own competency to manage a case committed to her care, *did not* send for a male physician as the law required. Although it was fully proved that she had done every thing that could have been done in the case, her penalty was imprisonment for twenty years. Two other cases are quoted by Dr. Schmidt, in which male practitioners were summoned before a legal tribunal, and it was proved that they *had not* done that which was necessary ; yet their penalty was no heavier than that inflicted on the woman, who had done exactly what she ought.

At this time (1818), it was also made illegal for any woman to practise who had not been educated. This brought the profession again into repute among women of the higher classes. A school for mid-

wives, supported by the government, was established
in Berlin, in which women have since continued to
be educated for practice in this city and in other
parts of Prussia. Two midwives are elected each
year, by a committee, from the applicants, to be
educated for practice in Berlin; and, as they have
to study two years, there are always four of these
students in the school, two graduating every year.
The remainder of the students are from the provin-
cial districts. To be admitted to this school is
considered a stroke of good fortune; as there are
generally more than a hundred applicants, many
of whom have to wait eight or ten years before
they are elected. There is, besides, a great deal of
favoritism; those women being generally chosen
who are the widows or wives of civil officers or
physicians; to whom this chance of earning a
livelihood is given, in order that they may not
become a burden on the government. Though
educated apart from the male students while
studying the theory of midwifery, they attend the
accouchement-ward together, and receive clinical
or practical instruction in the same class, from the
same professor.

The male students of medicine are admitted
to the university at the age of eighteen; having

first been required to go through a prescribed
course of collegiate study, and to pass the requisite
examination. Here they attend the lectures of
various professors, often of four or five upon the
same subject, in order to learn how it is treated
from different points of view. Then, after having
thus studied for a certain length of time, they
present themselves for an examination by the
professors of the university, which confers upon
them the title of " M.D.," without the right to
practise. They are then obliged to prepare for
what is called the State's examination, before a
Board of the most distinguished men in the profession, appointed to this place by the government:
these also constitute the medical court. Of this
number, Dr. Schmidt was one.

Dr. Schmidt approved my resolution, and expressed himself warmly in favor of it. He also
recommended to me a course of reading, to be
commenced at once, as a kind of preliminary education; and, although he had no influence with the
committee of the city government who examined
and elected the pupils, he promised to call upon
some of them, and urge my election. But, despite
his recommendation and my father's position as
civil officer, I received a refusal, on the grounds that

I was much too young (being only eighteen), and that I was unmarried. The latter fault I did not try to remove; the former I corrected daily; and, when I was nineteen, I repeated my application, and received the same reply. During this time, Dr. Schmidt became more and more interested in me personally. He promised that he would do all in his power to have me chosen the next year; while, during this time, he urged me to read and study as much as possible, in order to become fully acquainted with the subject. As usual, I continued to assist my mother in visiting her patients, and thus had a fine opportunity for explaining to myself many things which the mere study of books left in darkness. In fact, these years of preliminary practical study were more valuable to me than all the lectures that I ever listened to afterwards. Full of zeal and enthusiasm, and stimulated by a friend whose position and personal acquirements inspired me with reverence and devotion, I thought of nothing else than how to prepare myself in such a way that I should not disappoint him nor those to whom he had commended me. Dr. Schmidt was consumptive, and almost an invalid; often having to lecture in a reclining position. The author of many valuable medical works, and director of the

largest hospital in Prussia (the Charité of Berlin),
he found a most valuable assistant in his wife, —
one of the noblest women that ever lived. She
was always with him, except in the lecture-room;
and almost all of his works are said to have been
written by her from his dictation. This had inspired him with the highest possible respect for
women. He had the utmost faith in their powers
when rightly developed, and always declared their
intellectual capacity to be the same with that of
men. This belief inspired him with the desire to
give me an education superior to that of the common midwives; and, at the same time, to reform
the school of midwives by giving to it a professor
of its own sex. To this position he had in his own
mind already elected me; but, before I could take
it, I had to procure a legitimate election from the
city to the school as pupil; while, during my attendance, he had to convince the government of the
necessity of such a reform, as well as to bring over
the medical profession : which was not so easily
done; for many men were waiting already for Dr.
Schmidt's death in order to obtain this very post,
which was considered valuable.

When I was twenty, I received my third refusal.
Dr. Schmidt, whose health was failing rapidly, had

exerted himself greatly to secure my admission;
and the medical part of the committee had promised
him that they would give me their vote : but some
theological influence was set to work to elect one
of the deaconesses in my stead, that she might be
educated for the post of superintendent of the
lying-in ward of the hospital, which was under Dr.
Schmidt's care.   She also was rejected, in order
not to offend Dr. Schmidt ; but for this he would
not thank them.   No sooner had I carried him the
letter of refusal than he ordered his carriage, and,
proceeding to the royal palace, obtained an audience
of the king ; to whom he related the refusal of the
committee to elect me, on the ground that I was too
young and unmarried, and entreated of him a
cabinet order which should compel the city to admit me to the school ; adding, that he saw no reason
why Germany, as well as France, should not have
and be proud of a La Chapelle.   The king, who
held Dr. Schmidt in high esteem, gave him at once
the desired order ; and I became legally the student
of my friend : though his praise procured me intense vexation ; for my name was dropped entirely,
and I was only spoken of as La Chapelle the Second ; which would by no means have been unpleasant, had I earned the title ; but to receive it sneer-

ingly in advance, before having been allowed to
make my appearance publicly, was indeed unbearable.

On the third day after his visit to the king, Dr.
Schmidt received me into the class, and introduced
me to it as his future assistant teacher. This announcement was as surprising to me as to the class;
but I took it quietly, thinking that, if Dr. Schmidt
did not consider me fit for the place, he would not
risk being attacked for it by the profession *en masse*,
by whom he was watched closely.

On the same day, a little incident occurred which
I must mention. In the evening, instead of going
alone to the class for practical instruction, I accompanied Dr. Schmidt at his request. We entered
the hall where his assistant, the chief physician,
had already commenced his instructions. Dr.
Schmidt introduced me to him as his private pupil,
to whom he wished him to give particular attention; ending by giving my name. The physician
hurriedly came up to me, and grasped my hand,
exclaiming, "Why, this is my little blind doctor!"
I looked at him, and recognized the very Dr. Müller with whom I used to make the rounds of the
hospital when twelve years old, and who had since
risen to the position of chief physician. This ren-

contre, and the interest that he manifested afterwards, greatly relieved Dr. Schmidt, who had
feared that he would oppose me, instead of giving
me any special aid.   During this winter's study, I
spent the most of the time in the hospital, being
almost constantly at the side of Dr. Schmidt.   I
certainly made the most of every opportunity; and
I scarcely believe it possible for any student to
learn more in so short a time than I did during this
winter.   I was continually busy ; acting even as
nurse, whenever I could learn any thing by it.   During the following summer, I was obliged to reside
wholly in the hospital ; this being a part of the
prescribed education.   Here I became acquainted
with all the different wards, and had a fine opportunity to watch the cases by myself.   In the mean
time, Dr. Schmidt's illness increased so rapidly,
that he feared to die before his plans in respect to
me had been carried out ; especially as the state
of his health had compelled him to give up his position as Chief Director of the Hospital Charité.
His design was to make me chief accoucheuse in
the hospital, and to surrender into my hands his
position as professor in the School for Midwives, so
that I might have the entire charge of the midwives' education.   The opposition to this plan was

twofold : firstly, the theological influence that sought to place the deaconess (Sister Catherine) in the position of house-midwife ; and, secondly, the younger part of the profession, many of whom were anxious for the post of professor in the School for Midwives, which never would have been suffered to fall into the hands of Sister Catherine. Dr. Schmidt, however, was determined to yield to neither. Personal pride demanded that he should succeed in his plan ; and several of the older and more influential members of the profession took his part, among whom were Johannes Müller, Busch, Müller, Kilian, &c. During the second winter, his lecturing in the class was only nominal ; often nothing more than naming the heads of the subjects, while I had to give the real instruction. His idea was to make me feel the full responsibility of such a position, and, at the same time, to give me a chance to do the work that he had declared me pre-eminently capable of doing. This was an intrigue ; but he could not have it otherwise. He did not intend that I should perform his duty for his benefit, but for my own. He wished to show to the government the fact that I had done the work of a man like himself, and done it well ; and that, if he had not told them of his withdrawal, no one would have recognized his absence from the result.

At the close of this term, I was obliged to pass my examination at the same time with the fifty-six students who composed the class. Dr. Schmidt invited some of the most prominent medical men to be present, besides those appointed as the examining committee. He informed me of this on the day before the examination, saying, "I want to convince them that you can do better than half of the young men at *their* examination."

The excitement of this day I can hardly describe. I had not only to appear before a body of strangers, of whose manner of questioning I had no idea, but also before half a dozen authorities in the profession, assembled especially for criticism. Picture to yourself my position : standing before the table at which were seated the three physicians composing the examining committee, questioning me all the while in the most perplexing manner, with four more of the highest standing on each side, — making eleven in all ; Dr. Schmidt a little way off, anxious that I should prove true all that he had said in praise of me ; and the rest of the class in the background, filling up the large hall. It was terrible. The trifling honor of being considered capable was rather dearly purchased. I went through the whole hour bravely, without missing a single question; until finally the clock struck twelve, when every thing suddenly grew black before my eyes, and the last question sounded like a humming noise in my ear. I answered it, — how, I know not, — and was permitted to sit down and rest for fifteen minutes before I was called to the practical examination on the manikin. I gave satisfaction to all, and received the diploma of the first degree. This by no means ended the excitement. The students of the year were next examined. This examination continued for a week; after which the diplomas were announced, when it was found that never before had there been so many of the first degree, and so few of the third. Dr. Schmidt then made it known that this was the result of my exertions, and I was pronounced *a very capable woman.*

This acknowledgment having been made by the medical men present at the examination, Dr. Schmidt thought it would be an easy matter to get me installed into the position for which I had proved myself capable. But such could not be the case in a government ruled by hypocrisy and intrigue. To acknowledge the capability of a woman

5

did not by any means say that she was at liberty to hold a position in which she could exercise this capability. German men are educated to be slaves to the government: positive freedom is comprehended only by a few. They generally struggle for a kind of negative freedom; namely, for themselves: for each man, however much he may be inclined to show his subserviency to those superior in rank, thinks himself the lord of creation; and, of course, regards woman only as his appendage. How can this lord of creation, being a slave himself, look upon the *free development* and *demand of recognition* of his appendage otherwise than as a nonsense, or usurpation of his exclusive rights? And among these lords of creation I heartily dislike that class which not only yield to the influence brought upon them by government, but who also possess an infinite amount of narrowness and vanity, united to as infinite servility to money and position. There is not ink and paper enough in all the world to write down the contempt I feel for men in whose power it is to be free in thought and noble in action, and who act to the contrary to feed their ambition or their purses. I have learned, perhaps, too much of their spirit for my own good.

You can hardly believe what I experienced, in

respect to intrigue, within the few months following my examination. All the members of the medical profession were unwilling that a woman should take her place on a level with them. All the diplomatists became fearful that Dr. Schmidt intended to advocate the question of "woman's rights;" one of them exclaiming one evening, in the heat of discussion, "For Heaven's sake! the Berlin women are already wiser than all the men of Prussia: what will become of us if we allow them to manifest it?" I was almost forgotten in the five months during which the question was debated: it became more than a matter of personal intrigue. The real question at stake was, "How shall women be educated, and what is their true sphere?" and this was discussed with more energy and spirit than ever has been done here in America.

Scores of letters were written by Dr. Schmidt to convince the government that a woman could really be competent to hold the position in question, and that I had been pronounced so by the whole Faculty. The next objection raised was that my father was known as holding revolutionary principles; and to conquer this, cost a long discussion, with many interviews of the officials with my father and Dr. Schmidt. The next thing urged was that I was much *too young;* that it would be necessary, in the course of my duties, to instruct the young men also ; and that there was danger in our thus being thrown together. In fact, this reason, read to me by Dr. Schmidt from one of the letters written at this time (all of which are still carefully preserved), runs thus : "To give this position to Miss M. E. Zakrzewska is dangerous. She is a prepossessing young lady; and, from coming in contact with so many gentlemen, must necessarily fall in love with some one of them, and thus end her career." To this I have only to reply, that I am sorry that I could not have found *one* among them that could have made me follow the suggestion. This objection, however, seemed for a while the most difficult to·be met : for it was well known, that, when a student myself, I had stood on the most friendly terms with my fellow-students, and that they had often taken my part in little disturbances that naturally came up in an establishment where no one was permitted to enter or to leave without giving a reason, and where even my private patients were sent away at the door because I did not know of their coming, and could not announce to the doorkeeper the name and residence of those who might possibly call.

That this difficulty was finally conquered, I have
to thank the students themselves. My relation
with these young men was of the pleasantest kind.
They never seemed to think that I was not of their
sex, but always treated me like one of themselves.
I knew of their studies and their amusements;
yes, even of the mischievous pranks that they
were planning both for college and for social life.
They often made me their confidante in their private affairs, and were more anxious for my approval
or forgiveness than for that of their relatives. I
learned, during this time, how great is the friendly
influence of a woman even upon fast-living and
licentious young men; and this has done more to
convince me of the necessity that the two sexes
should live together from infancy, than all the
theories and arguments that are brought to convince the mass of this fact. As soon as it became
known among the students that my youth was the
new objection, they treated it in such a manner that
the whole thing was transformed into a ridiculous
bugbear, growing out of the imagination of the
virtuous opposers.

Nothing now seemed left in the way of my attain-
ing to the position; when suddenly it dawned upon
the mind of some that I was irreligious; that neither

my father nor my mother attended church; and that, under such circumstances, I could not, of course, be a church-goer. Fortunately, I had complied with the requirements of the law, and could therefore bring my certificate of confirmation from one of the Protestant churches. By the advice of Dr. Schmidt, I commenced to attend church regularly, and continued until a little incident happened which I must relate here. One Sunday, just after the sermon was over, I remembered that I had forgotten to give instructions to the nurse in respect to a patient, and left the church without waiting for the end of the service. The next morning, I was summoned to answer to the charge of leaving the church at an improper time. The inquisitor (who was one of those who had accused me of irreligion), being vexed that I contradicted him by going to church regularly, was anxious to make me confess that I did not care for the service: but I saw through his policy as well as his hypocrisy, and simply told him the truth; namely, that I had forgotten important business, and therefore thought it excusable to leave as soon as the sermon was over. Whether he sought to lure me on to further avowals, I know not: but, whatever was his motive, he asked me, in reply, whether I believed that he cared for the humdrum custom of church-going, and whether I thought him imbecile enough to consider this as any thing more than the means by which to keep the masses in check ; adding, that it was the duty of the intelligent to make the affair respectable by setting the example of going themselves ; and that he only wished me to act on this principle, when all accusations of irreligion would fall to the ground. I had always known that this man was not my friend : but, when I heard this, I felt disenchanted with the whole world ; for I had never thought him more than a hypocrite, whereas I found him the meanest of Jesuits, both in theory and practice. I was thoroughly indignant ; the more so, since I felt guilty myself in going to church simply to please Dr. Schmidt. I do not remember what answer I gave ; but I know that my manners and words made it evident that I considered him a villain. He never forgave me this, as all his future acts proved to me : for, in his position of chief director of the hospital, he had it in his power, more than any one else, to annoy me ; and that he did so, you will presently see.

The constant opposition and attendant excitement, together with the annoyances which my father, as civil officer, had to endure, made him resolve to present a declaration to the government, that I should never, with his consent, enter the position. He had become so tired of my efforts to become a public character in my profession, that he suddenly conceived the wish to have me married. Now, take for a moment into consideration the facts that I was but twenty-two years of age, full of sanguine enthusiasm for my vocation, and strong in the friendship of Dr. Schmidt. He had inspired me with the idea of a career different from the common routine of domestic life. My mother, overcoming her repugnance to my entering my profession, had been my best friend, encouraging me steadily; while my father, yielding to the troubles that it involved, had become disgusted with it, and wished me to abandon my career. He was stern, and would not take back his word. I could do nothing without his consent; while Dr. Schmidt had finally overcome all difficulties, and had the prospect of victory if my father would but yield. A few weeks of this life were sufficient to drive one mad, and I am sure that I was near becoming so. I was resolved to run away from home or to kill myself, while my father was equally resolved to marry me to a man of whom I did not know the sight. Matters finally came to a crisis through the illness

of Dr. Schmidt, whose health failed so rapidly, that
it was thought dangerous to let him be longer excited by the fear of not realizing his favorite scheme.
Some of his medical advisers influenced the government to appeal to my father to withdraw his declaration; which, satisfied with the honor thus done
him, he did on the 1st of May, 1852. On the
15th of May, I received my legal instalment to
the position for which Dr. Schmidt had designed
me. The joy that I felt was great beyond expression. A youthful enthusiast of twenty-two, I stood
at the height of my wishes and expectations. I had
obtained what others only could obtain after the
protracted labor of half a lifetime; and already I
saw myself in imagination occupying the place
of Dr. Schmidt's aspirations, — that of a German
La Chapelle. No one, that has not passed at the
same age through the same excitement, can ever
comprehend the fulness of my rejoicing, which
was not wholly selfish; for I knew that nothing in
the world would please Dr. Schmidt so much as
this victory. The wildest joy of an accepted
suitor is a farce compared to my feelings on the
morning of that 15th of May. I was reconciled to
my bitterest opponents: I could even have thanked
them for their opposition, since it had made the

success so much the sweeter. Not the slightest
feeling of triumph was in my heart; all was happiness and rejoicing: and it was in this condition
of mind and heart that I put on my bonnet and
shawl to carry the good news to Dr. Schmidt.
Without waiting to be announced, I hastened to
his parlor, where I found him sitting with his wife
upon the sofa. I did not walk, but flew, towards
them, and threw the letter upon the table, exclaiming, " There is the victory!" Like a confla-
gration, my joy spread to Dr. Schmidt as well as to
his wife, who thought that she saw in these tidings
a cup of new life for her husband. I only staid
long enough to accept their congratulations. Dr.
Schmidt told me to be sure to come the next
morning to enter legally upon my duties at his
side. Meanwhile, he gave me a vacation for the
afternoon to see my friends and carry them the
news. He saw that I needed the open air, and
felt that he, too, must have it to counteract his joy.
I went to tell my father and several friends, and
spent the day in blissful ignorance of the dreadful
event that was transpiring.

The next morning, at seven o'clock, I left home
to go to my residence in the hospital. I had not
slept during the night: the youthful fire of enthu-

siasm burnt too violently to allow me any rest.
The old doorkeeper opened the door for me, and
gazed at me with an air of surprise. "What is the
matter?" I asked. "I am astonished to see you
so cheerful," said he. "Why?" I asked with
astonishment. "Don't you know that Dr. Schmidt
is dead?" was the answer. Dr. Schmidt dead!
I trembled; I staggered; I fell upon a chair. The
beautiful entrance-hall, serving also as a green-
house during the winter, filled in every place with
flowers and tropical fruit, faded from my eyes; and
in its stead I saw nothing but laughing faces, dis-
torted with scorn and mockery. A flood of tears
cooled the heat of my brain, and a calmness like
that of death soon took possession of me. I had
fallen from the topmost height of joy and happiness
to the profoundest depth of disappointment and despair. If there were nothing else to prove the
strength of my mind, the endurance of this sudden
change would be sufficient.

I went at once to Dr. Schmidt's residence in the
Hospital Park, where I met him again, not as I
had expected an hour before, ready to go with me to
the hospital-department which I was henceforth
to superintend, but a corpse. After I had left the
day before, he had expressed a wish to go into

the open air, he being not much less excited than
myself. Mrs. Schmidt ordered the carriage, and
they drove to the large park. He talked constantly
and excitedly about the satisfaction that he felt in
this success, until they arrived; when he wished to
get out of the carriage, and walk with his wife.
Mrs. Schmidt consented; but they had scarcely
taken a few steps when he sank to the ground,
and a gush of blood from his mouth terminated his
existence.

I left Dr. Schmidt's house, and entered alone
into the wards, where I felt that I was without
friendly encouragement and support. During the
three days that intervened before the burial of Dr.
Schmidt, I was hardly conscious of any thing, but
moved about mechanically like an automaton. The
next few days were days of confusion; for the
death of Dr. Schmidt had left so many places va-
cant, that some fifty persons were struggling to
obtain some one of his offices. The eagerness,
servility, and meanness which these educated men
displayed in striving to conquer their rivals was
more than disgusting. The serpents that lie in
wait for their prey are endurable; for we know
that it is their nature to be cunning and relentless:
but to see men of intellect and education sly and

snaky, ferocious, yet servile to the utmost, makes one almost believe in total depravity. The most of these men got what they deserved ; namely, nothing : the places were filled temporarily with others, and every thing went on apparently as before. My position soon became very disagreeable. I had received my instalment, not because I was wanted by the directors of the hospital, but because they had been commanded by the government to accept me in the hope of thus prolonging the life of Dr. Schmidt. Young and inexperienced in petty intrigue, I had now to work without friendly encouragement and appreciation, with no one about me in whom I had a special interest ; while every one was regretting that the instalment had been given me before Dr. Schmidt's death, which might have happened just as well from some other excitement, in an establishment where three thousand people were constantly at war about each other's affairs. I surveyed the whole arena, and saw very well, that, unless I practised meanness and dishonesty as well as the rest, I could not remain there for any length of time ; for scores were ready to calumniate me whenever there was the least thing to be gained by it.

I was about to commence a new period of life.

I had a solid structure as a foundation; but the
superstructure had been built up in so short a time,
that a change of wind would suffice to cast it down.
I resolved, therefore, to tear it down myself, and to
begin to build another upon the carefully laid basis;
and only waited for an opportunity to manifest my
intention. This opportunity soon presented itself.
Sister Catherine, the deaconess of whom I have
spoken, who had been allowed to attend the School
of Midwives after my election, through the influence
of her theological friends upon Dr. Schmidt (the
city magistrates having refused her because I was
already the third accepted pupil), had as yet no
position : and these friends now sought to make her
the second *accoucheuse;* I having the first position,
with the additional title of Chief. This she would
not accept. She, the experienced deaconess, who
had been a Florence Nightingale in the typhus
epidemic of Silesia, was unwilling to be under the
supervision of a woman who had nothing to show
but a thorough education, and who was, besides,
eight years younger than herself. Her refusal
made my enemies still more hostile. Why they
were so anxious for her services, I can only explain by supposing that the directors of the hospital
wished to annoy Pastor Fliedner, the originator of

the Kaiserswerth Sisterhood; for, in placing Sister Catherine in this position, they robbed him of one of the very best nurses that he ever had in his institution.

My desire. to reconcile the government of the hospital, in order that I might have peace in my position to pursue my development and education so as to realize and manifest to the people the truth of what Dr. Schmidt had affirmed of me, induced me to go to one of the directors, and propose that Sister Catherine should be installed on equal terms with me; offering to drop the title of Chief, and to consent that the department should be divided into two. My proposition was accepted nominally, and Sister Catherine was installed, but with a third less salary than I received; while I had to give the daily reports, &c., and to take the chief responsibility of the whole. Catherine was quite friendly to me; and I was happy in the thought that there was now one at least who would stand by me, should any difficulties occur. How much I was mistaken in the human heart! This pious, sedate woman, towards whom my heart yearned with friendship, was my greatest enemy; though I did not know it until after my arrival in America.

A few weeks afterwards, the city petitioned to have a number of women instructed in the practice of midwifery. These women were all experienced nurses, who had taken the liberty to practise this art to a greater or less extent from what they had learned of it while nursing; and, to put an end to this unlawful practice, they had been summoned before an examining committee, and the youngest and best educated chosen to be instructed as the law required.   Dr. Müller, the pathologist, was appointed to superintend the theoretical, and Dr. Ebert the practical, instruction.   Dr. Müller, who never had given this kind of instruction before, and who was a special friend of mine, immediately surrendered the whole into my hands; while Dr. Ebert, whose time was almost wholly absorbed in the department of the diseases of children, appointed me as his assistant.   Both gentlemen gave me certificates of this when I determined to emigrate to America.

The marked preference for my wards that had always been shown by the male students was shared by these women when they came.   Sister Catherine was neither ambitious nor envious; yet she felt that she was the second in place.   Drs. Müller and Ebert never addressed themselves to her; neither did they impress the nurses and the servants with the idea that she was any thing more than the head-nurse. All these things together made her a spy; and, though nothing happened for which I could be reproved, all that I said and did was watched and secretly reported. Under a despotic government, the spy is as necessary as the corporal. The annoyance of this reporting is, that the secrecy exists only for the one whom it concerns; while the subaltern officers and servants receive hints that such a person is kept under constant surveillance. When it was found that no occasion offered to find fault with me, our administrative inspector was removed, and a surly old corporal put in his place, with the hint that the government of the hospital thought that the former inspector did not perform his duty rightly, since he never reported disturbance in a ward that had been notorious as being the most disorderly in former times. The truth was, that, in my innocence of heart, I had been striving to gain the respect and friendship of my enemies by doing my work better than any before me had done. To go to bed at night regularly was a thing unknown to me. Once I was not undressed for twenty-one days and nights; superintending and giving instructions on six or eight confinement cases

in every twenty-four hours ; lecturing three hours
every afternoon to the class of midwives ; giving
clinical lectures to them twice a week, for an hour
in the morning; superintending the care of some
twenty infants, who were epidemically attacked with
purulent ophthalmia ; and having, besides, the general supervision of the whole department. But
all this could not overcome the hostility of my enemies, the chief cause of which lay in the mortifica-
tion at having been vanquished by my appointment.
On the other hand, I was happy in the thought that
Mrs. Schmidt continued to take the same interest
in me as before, and was glad to hear of my partial
success. The students, both male and female, were
devoted to me, and manifested their gratitude openly
and frankly. This was the greatest compensation
that I received for my work. The women wished
to show their appreciation by paying me for the
extra labor that I performed in their instruction ;
not knowing the fact, that I did it simply in
order that they might pass an examination which
should again convince the committee that I was in
the right place. I forbade them all payment, as I
had refused it to the male students when they
wished to pay me for their extra instruction on the
manikin : but in a true, womanly way, they ma-

naged to learn the date of my birthday; when two or
three, instead of attending the lecture, took possession of my room, which they decorated with flowers;
while on the table they displayed presents to the
amount of some hundred and twenty dollars, which
the fifty-six women of the class had collected among
themselves. This was, of course, a great surprise to
me, and really made me feel sad; for I did not
wish for things of this sort. I wished to prove that
unselfishness was the real motive of my work; and
thought that I should finally earn the crown of
appreciation from my enemies, for which I was
striving. This gift crossed all my plans. I must
accept it, if I would not wound the kindest of hearts;
yet I felt that I lost my game by so doing. I
quietly packed every thing into a basket, and put it
out of sight under the bed, in order that I might
not be reminded of my loss. Of course, all these
things were at once reported. I saw in the faces of
many that something was in agitation, and waited
a fortnight in constant expectation of its coming.
But these people wished to crush me entirely. They
knew well that a blow comes hardest when least
expected, and therefore kept quiet week after week,
until I really began to ask their pardon in my heart
for having done them the wrong to expect them to

act meanly about a thing that was natural and allowable. In a word, I became quiet and happy again in the performance of my duties; until suddenly, six weeks after my birthday, I was summoned to the presence of Director Horn (the same who had reprimanded me for leaving the church), who received me with a face as hard and stern as an avenging judge, and asked me whether I knew that it was against the law to receive any other payment than that given me by the hospital. Upon my avowing that I did, he went on to ask how it was, then, that I had accepted gifts on my birthday. This question fell upon me like a thunderbolt; for I never had thought of looking upon these as a payment. Had these women paid me for the instruction that I gave them beyond that which was prescribed, they ought each one to have given me the value of the presents. I told him this in reply, and also how disagreeable the acceptance had been to me, and how ready I was to return the whole at his command; since it had been my desire to prove, not only my capability, but my unselfishness in the work. The man was ashamed; I saw it in his face as he turned it away from me: yet he saw in me a proof that he had been vanquished in intrigue, and was resolved that the occasion should end in my overthrow. Much more was said about the presents and their significance; and I soon ceased to be the humble woman, and spoke boldly what I thought, in defiance of his authority, as I had done at the time of the religious conversation (by the way, I never attended church again after that interview). The end was, that I declared my readiness to leave the hospital. He wished to inflict direct punishment on me; and forbade me to be present at the examination of the class, which was to take place the next day. This was really a hard penalty, to which he was forced for his own sake; for, if I had been present, I should have told the whole affair to men of a nobler stamp, who would have opposed, as they afterwards did, my leaving a place which I filled to their entire satisfaction.

I made my preparations to leave the hospital on the 15th of November. What was I to do? I was not made to practise quietly, as is commonly done: my education and aspirations demanded more than this. For the time, I could do nothing more than inform my patients that I intended to practise independently. My father again wished that I should marry; and I began to ask myself, whether marriage is an institution to relieve pa-

rents from embarrassment. When troubled about
the future of a son, parents are ready to give him
to the army; when in fears of the destiny of a
daughter, they induce her to become the slave of
the marriage bond. I never doubted that it was
more unendurable and unworthy to be a wife without love, than a soldier without a special calling
for that profession; and I never could think of
marriage as the means to procure a shelter and
bread.

I had so many schemes in my head, that I would
not listen to his words. Among these was especially the wish to emigrate to America. The Penn-
sylvania Female Medical College had sent its first
Report to Dr. Schmidt, who had informed me of it
as well as his colleagues, and had advocated the
justice of such a reform. This fact occurred to
my memory; and, for the next two months, I did
nothing but speculate how to carry out my design
of emigration. I had lived rather expensively and
lavishly, without thinking of laying up any money;
and my whole fortune, when I left the Charité, consisted of sixty dollars.

One thing happened in connection with my leaving the hospital, which I must relate here. Director Horn was required to justify his conduct to

the minister to whom the change had to be reported ;
and a committee was appointed to hear the accusa-
tion, and pass judgment upon the affair. As this
was done in secrecy and not before a jury, and as
the accuser was a man of high rank, I knew nothing
of it until Christmas Eve, when I received a docu-
ment, stating that, *as a gratification for my services
for the benefit of the city of Berlin* in instructing the
class of midwives, a compensation was decreed me
of fifty dollars. This was a large sum for Berlin,
such as was only given on rare occasions. I was
also informed that Director Horn was instructed to
give me, should I ever demand it, a first-class certificate of what my position had been in the hospital, with the title of Chief attached. Whatever I
had suffered from the injustice of my enemies,
I was now fully recompensed. I inquired who
had taken my part so earnestly against Director
Horn as to gain this action, and found that it was
Dr. Müller the pathologist, backed by several
other physicians. Director Horn, it was said, was
greatly humiliated by the decision of Minister von
Raumer, who could not see the least justice in his
conduct in this matter ; and, had I not left the
hospital so readily, I should never have stood so
firmly as after this secret trial.

It was done, however; and I confidently told my
mother of my design to emigrate. Between my
mother and myself there existed, not merely the
strongest relation of maternal and filial love, but also
a professional sympathy and peculiar friendship,
which was the result of two similar minds and hearts,
and which made me stand even nearer to her than
as a child I could possibly have done. She consented
with heart and soul, encouraged me in all my plans
and expectations, and asked me at once at what
time I would leave. I next told my father and the
rest of the family of my plan. My third sister
(Anna), a beautiful, joyous young girl, exclaimed,
"And I will go with you!" My father, who
would not listen to my going alone, at once consented to our going together. But I thought dif-
ferently. In going alone, I risked only my own
happiness: in going with her, I risked hers too;
while I should be constantly restricted in my ad-
venturous undertaking from having her with me,
who knew nothing of the world save the happiness
of a tranquil family life. The next day, I told
them that I had changed my mind, and should not
go away, but should establish myself in Berlin.
Of course, I received a torrent of gibes on my fic-
kleness; for they did not understand my feelings in

respect to the responsibility that I feared to take for my younger sister.

I began to establish myself in practice. Mrs. Schmidt, who was anxious to assist me in my new career, suggested to those physicians who were my friends the establishment of a private hospital, which should be under my care. She found them strongly in favor of the plan ; and, had I not been constantly speculating about leaving for America, this scheme would have been realized. But I had resolved to emigrate, and took my measures accordingly. I went secretly to Drs. Müller and Ebert, and procured certificates from them attesting my position in respect to them in the hospital. I then obtained the certificate from Director Horn, and carried them all to the American Chargé d'Affaires (Theodore S. Fay) to have them legalized in English, so that they, could be of service to me in America.*

---

* "The undersigned, Secretary of Legation of the United States of America, certifies that Miss Marie Elizabeth Zakrzewska has exhibited to him very strong recommendations from the highest professional authorities of Prussia, as a scientific, practical, experienced *accoucheuse* of unusual talent and skill. She has been chief *accoucheuse* in the Royal Hospital of Berlin, and possesses a certificate of her superiority from the Board of Directors of that institution. She has not only manifested great

When I told Drs. Ebert and Müller and Mrs.
Schmidt of my intention to emigrate, they pronounced me insane. They thought that I had the
best field of activity open in Berlin, and could not
comprehend why I should seek greater freedom of
person and of action. Little really is known in
Berlin about America, and to go there is considered as great an undertaking as to seek the river
Styx in order to go to Hades. The remark that I
heard from almost every quarter was, "What! you
wish to go to the land of barbarism, where they have
negro slavery, and where they do not know how to
appreciate talent and genius?" But this could not
prevent me from realizing my plans. I had idealized the freedom of America, and especially the
reform of the position of women, to such an extent,
that I would not listen to their arguments. After

---

talent as a practitioner, but also as a teacher; and enjoys the
advantage of a moral and irreproachable private character.
She has attained this high rank over many female competitors
in the same branch; there being more than fifty † in the city of
Berlin who threaten, by their acknowledged excellence, to mo-
nopolize the obstetric art.   " THEO. S. FAY.

" LEGATION UNITED STATES, BERLIN, Jan. 26, 1853."

[SEAL.]

---

† " Upon inquiry, I find that, instead of fifty, there are one hundred
and ten female *accoucheuses* in Berlin.   " THEO. S. FAY."

having been several years in America, very probably I would think twice before undertaking again
to emigrate; for even the idealized freedom has
lost a great deal of its charm, when I consider how
much better it could be.

Having put every thing in order, I told my father
of my conclusion to leave. He was surprised to
hear of it the second time: but I showed him my
papers in readiness for the journey, and declared
that I should go as soon as the ship was ready to sail;
having a hundred dollars, — just money enough to
pay my passage. He would not give his consent,
unless my sister Anna accompanied me; thinking
her, I suppose, a counterpoise to any rash undertakings in which I might engage in a foreign land.
If I wished to go, I was, therefore, forced to have
her company; of which I should have been very
glad, had I not feared the moral care and responsibility. We decided to go in a fortnight. My
father paid her passage, and gave her a hundred
dollars in cash, — just enough to enable us to spend
a short time in New York: after which he expected
either to send us more money, or that we would
return; and, in case we did this, an agreement was
made with the shipping-merchant that payment
should be made on our arrival in Hamburg.

On the 13th of March, 1853, we left the paternal roof, to which we should never return. My mother bade us adieu with tears in her eyes; saying, "*Au revoir* in America!" She was determined to follow us.

Dear Mary, here ends my Berlin and European life; and I can assure you that this was the hardest moment I ever knew. Upon my memory is for ever imprinted the street, the house, the window behind which my mother stood waving her handkerchief. Not a tear did I suffer to mount to my eyes, in order to make her believe that the departure was an easy one; but a heart beating convulsively within punished me for the restraint.

. My father and brothers accompanied us to the *dépôt*, where the cars received us for Hamburg. On our arrival there, we found that the ice had not left the Elbe, and that the ships could not sail until the river was entirely free. We were forced to remain three weeks in Hamburg. We had taken staterooms in the clipper ship "Deutschland." Besides ourselves, there were sixteen passengers in the first cabin; people good enough in their way, but not sufficiently attractive to induce us to make their acquaintance. We observed a dead silence as to who we were, where we were going, or what was the motive of our emigrating to America. The only person that we ever spoke to was a Mr. R. from Hamburg, a youth of nineteen, who, like ourselves, had left a happy home in order to try his strength in a strange land. The voyage was of forty-seven days' duration; excessively stormy, but otherwise very dull, like all voyages of this kind; and, had it not been for the expectations that filled our hearts, we should have died of *ennui.* As it was, the days passed slowly, made worse by the inevitable sea-sickness of our fellow-passengers; and we longed for the hour that should bring us in sight of the shores of the New World. And now commences *my life in America.*

"Dear Marie, best Marie! make haste to come upon deck to see America! Oh, how pleasant it is to see the green trees again! How brightly the sun is gilding the land you are seeking, — the land of freedom!" With such childlike exclamations of delight, my sister Anna burst into my cabin to hasten my appearance on deck on the morning of the 22d of May, 1853. The beautiful child of nineteen summers was only conscious of a heart overflowing with pleasure at the sight of the charming landscape that opened before her eyes after a tedious voyage of forty-seven days upon the ocean.

We had reached the quarantine at Staten Island. The captain, the old pilot, every one, gazed at her as she danced joyously about the deck, with a mingled feeling of sadness and curiosity; for our reserve while on shipboard had surrounded us with a sort of mystery which none knew how to unravel.

As soon as I had dressed for going on shore, and had packed up the things that we had used on our voyage, in order that they might not be stolen during this time of excitement, I obeyed the last call of my impatient sister to come at least to see the last rays of sunrise; and went on deck, where I was at once riveted by the beautiful scene that was spread before my eyes. The green, sloping lawns, with which the white cottages formed such a cheerful contrast; the trees, clad in their first foliage, and suggesting hope by their smiling blossoms; the placid cows, feeding quietly in the fields; the domestic chickens, just visible in the distance; and the friendly barking of a dog, — all seemed to greet me with a first welcome to the shores of this strange country: while the sun, shining brightly from a slightly clouded sky, mellowed the whole landscape, and so deeply impressed my soul, that tears sprang to my eyes, and a feeling rose in my heart that I can call nothing else than devotional;

for it bowed my knees beneath me, and forced
sounds from my lips that I could not translate into
words, for they were mysterious to myself. A
stranger in a strange, wide land, not knowing its
habits and customs, not understanding its people,
not yet understanding its workings and aims, my
mind was not clouded with loneliness. I was happy. Had it not been my own wish that had made
me leave the home of a kind father, and of a
mother beloved beyond all earthly beings? I had
succeeded in safely reaching the shores of America. Life was again open before me. With these
thoughts, I turned from the beautiful landscape;
and finding the captain, a noble-hearted sailor, inquired of him how long it would take us to reach
the port of New York. "That is New York,"
said he, pointing to a dark mass of buildings, with
here and there a spire towering in the air. "We
shall reach there about eight o'clock; but it is
Sunday, and you will have to stay on board till
to-morrow." With this he turned away, calling
his men to weigh anchor; as the physician, whose
duty it was to inspect the cargo of men, like cattle,
had just left in his boat. On we went, my sister
still dancing and singing for joy; and Mr. R. and
myself sitting somewhat apart, — he looking de-

'spondently into the water, I with my head firmly raised in the air, happy in heart, but thoughtful in mind, and trusting in my inward strength for the future.

I took my breakfast on deck. No one seemed to have any appetite ; and I felt somewhat reproved when I heard some one near me say, "She seems to have neither head nor heart : see how tranquilly she can eat at such a time as this!" These words were spoken by one of the cabin-passengers, — a young man, who was exceedingly curious to know why I was going to America, and had several times tried to make the rest of the passengers believe that it must be in consequence of an unhappy love. The poor simpleton ! he thought that women could only enter into life through the tragedy of a broken heart.

A bell sounded. We were opposite Trinity Church, which had just struck eight. On my right lay an enormous collection of bricks (houses I could not call them ; for, seen from the ship, they resembled only a pile of ruins) ; on my left, the romantic shore of New Jersey. But the admiration with which I had gazed upon Staten Island was gone as I stood before this beautiful scene ; the appreciation of Nature was mastered by another feeling, — a feeling

of activity that had become my ideal. I had come
here for a purpose, — to carry out the plan which
a despotic government and its servile agents had
prevented me from doing in my native city. I had
to show to those men who had opposed me so
strongly because I was a woman, that in this land of
liberty, equality, and fraternity, I could maintain
that position which they would not permit to me at
home. My talents were in an unusual direction. I
was a physician; and, as such, had for years moved
in the most select circles of Berlin. Even my enemies had been forced to give me the highest testi-
monials: and these were the only treasure that I
brought to this country; for I had given my last
dollar to the sailor who brought me the first news
that land was in sight.

I looked again upon New York, but with a feeling that a great mystery was lying before my
eyes, — a feeling that was confirmed by the men,
who came off to the ship in small boats, speaking
a language that seemed like a chaos of sounds.
As I turned, I saw my sister coming slowly up from
the cabin with a changed air; and I asked her with
surprise what was the matter. "O Marie!" said
she, "most of the passengers are called for. Mr.
R.'s brother has just come to take him on shore.

7

He was so glad to see him (for he thought he was in New Orleans), that I think he will forget to say good-by. I am afraid that we shall have to stay here all alone, and" —— " Are the Misses· Zakrzewska on board?" called a voice from a little boat by the side of the ship. We looked down in surprise, but did not recognize the man, who spoke as if he were an acquaintance. The captain answered, " Yes." Upon which the same voice said, " Mr. G. requests them to wait: he will be here in a moment."

This announcement surprised us the more that it came from a totally unexpected quarter. An acquaintance of ours, who had emigrated to New York a few years before, and had shortly after married a Mr. G., had heard from her brother in Berlin of our departure for America in the ship " Deutschland; " and these good people, thinking that they could be of use to us in a new country, had been watching for its arrival. No one on board dared ask a question as to who our friends were, so reserved had we been in regard to our plans: only the young man who had accused me of having neither head nor heart said, half aside, " Ah, ha! now we know the reason why Miss Marie ate her breakfast so calmly, while her sister

danced for joy. They had beaux who were expecting them." "Simpleton!" thought I: "must
women always have beaux in order to be calm about
the future?"

Mr. G. came on board in a few minutes, bringing us from his wife an invitation of welcome to
her house. I cannot express in words the emotion
awakened in my heart by the really unselfish kindness that had impelled these people to greet us in
this manner; and this was increased when we
reached their very modest dwelling, consisting of
a large shop in which Mr. G. carried on his
business of manufacturing fringes and tassels, one
sitting-room, a bedroom, and a small kitchen. My
strength left me, and my composure dissolved in a
flood of tears. The good people did all that they
could to make us feel at home, and insisted that
we should occupy the sitting-room until we had
decided what further to do. Of course, I determined that this should be for as short a time as
possible, and that we would immediately look out
for other lodgings.

One-half of this first day was spent in talking
about home; the other, in making an excursion to
Hoboken. This visit we would gladly have dis-
pensed with, so exhausted were we by the excite-

ment that we had passed through since sunrise; but our friends were bent on entertaining us with stories and sights of the New World, and we followed them rather reluctantly. I have since been glad that I did so; for my mind was in a state that rendered it far more impressible than usual, and therefore better fitted to observe much that would have been lost to me in a less-excited condition. Here I first saw the type of common German life on Sunday in America; and I saw enough of it on that one Sunday afternoon to last a whole lifetime. My friends called on several of their acquaintances. Everywhere that we went, I noticed two peculiarities, — comparative poverty in the surroundings, and apparent extravagance in the manner of living: for in every house we found an abundance of wine, beer, cake, meat, salad, &c., although it was between the hours of meals; and every one was eating, although no one seemed hungry. At nine o'clock in the evening, the visit was concluded by going to a hotel, where a rich supper was served up to us; and at eleven at night we returned home. My work in America had already commenced. Was it not necessary for a stranger in a new country to observe life in all its phases, before entering upon it? It seemed so to me; and I had already

planned, while on ship-board, to spend the first
month in observations of this kind. I had made a
fair beginning; and, when I saw many repetitions
of this kind of life among my countrymen, I feared
that this was their main purpose in this country,
and their consolation for the loss of the entertain-
ments and recreations which their fatherland offered to them. But, as soon as I got opportunity
to make my observations among the educated classes, I found my fear ungrounded; and I also found
that the Americans had noticed the impulse for
progress and higher development which animated
these Germans. The German mind, so much
honored in Europe for its scientific capacity, for
its consistency regarding principles, and its correct
criticism, is not dead here : but it has to struggle
against difficulties too numerous to be detailed
here; and therefore it is that the Americans don't
know of its existence, and the chief obstacle is
their different languages. A Humboldt must remain unknown here, unless he chooses to Ameri-
canize himself in every respect; and could he do
this without ceasing to be Humboldt the cosmo-
politan genius?

It would be a great benefit to the development
of this country if the German language was made

a branch of education, and not an accomplishment simply. Only then would the Americans appreciate how much has been done by the Germans to advance higher development, and to diffuse the true principles of freedom. It would serve both parties to learn how much the Germans aid in developing the reason, and supporting progress in every direction. The revolution of 1848 has been more serviceable to America than to Germany; for it has caused the emigration of thousands of men who would have been the pride of a free Germany. America has received the German freemen, whilst Germany has retained the *subjects*.

The next morning, I determined to return to the ship to look after my baggage. As Mr. and Mrs. G. were busy in their shop, there was no one to accompany me : I therefore had either to wait until they were at leisure, or to go alone. I chose the latter, and took my first walk in the city of New York on my way to the North River, where the ship was lying. The noise and bustle everywhere about me absorbed my attention to such a degree, that, instead of turning to the right hand, I went to the left, and found myself at the East River, in the neighborhood of Peek Slip. Here I inquired after the German ship "Deutschland," and was directed, in my native tongue, down to the Battery, and thence up to Pier 13, where I found the ship discharging the rest of her passengers and their baggage. It was eleven o'clock when I reached the ship: I had, therefore, taken a three-hours' walk. I had now to wait until the custom-house officer had inspected my trunks, and afterwards for the arrival of Mr. G., who came at one o'clock with a cart to convey the baggage to his house. While standing amidst the crowd, a man in a light suit of clothes of no positive color, with a complexion of the same sort, came up to me, and asked, in German, whether I had yet found a boarding-place. The man's smooth face instinctively repelled me; yet the feeling that I was not independently established made me somewhat indefinite in my reply. On seeing this, he at once grew talkative and friendly, and, speaking of the necessity of finding a safe and comfortable home, said that he could recommend me to a hotel where I would be treated honestly; or that, if I chose to be in a private family, he knew of a very kind, motherly lady, who kept a boarding-house for ladies alone, — not to make money, but for the sake of her country-women. The familiarity that he mingled in his

conversation while trying to be friendly made me
thoroughly indignant : I turned my back upon him,
saying that I did not need his services. It was not
long before I saw him besieging my sister Anna,
who had come with Mr. G.; being nervous lest I
might not have found the ship. What he said to
her, I do not know. I only remember that she
came to me, saying, "I am afraid of that man : I
wish that we could go home soon." This meeting
with a man who makes friendly offers of service
may seem a small matter to the mere looker-on ; but
it ceases to be so when one knows his motives : and,
since that time, I have had but too many opportunities to see for what end these offers are made.
Many an educated girl comes from the Old World
to find a position as governess or teacher, who is
taken up in this manner, and is never heard from
again, or is only found in the most wretched condition. It is shameful that the most effective
arrangements should not be made for the safety of
these helpless beings, who come to these shores with
the hope of finding a Canaan.

The week was mostly spent in looking for apartments ; as we had concluded to commence housekeeping on a small scale, in order to be more
independent and to save money. On our arrival,

I had borrowed from my sister the hundred dollars which my father had given her on our departure from Berlin, and which was to be my capital until I had established myself in business. I succeeded in finding a suite of rooms, with windows facing the street, in the house of a grocer; and, having put them in perfect order, we moved into them on the 6th of June, paying eleven dollars as our rent for two months in advance.

My sister took charge of our first day's housekeeping, while I went to deliver my letters of introduction. I went first to Dr. Reisig, in Fourteenth Street. My mother, who had employed him when he was a young man and we were small children, had spoken of him kindly; and, for this reason, I had confidence in him. I found him a very friendly man, but by no means a cordial one. He informed me that female physicians in this country were of the lowest rank, and that they did not hold even the position of a good nurse. He said that he wished to be of service to me if I were willing to serve as nurse; and, as he was just then in need of a good one, would recommend me for the position. I thanked him for his candor and kindness, but refused his offer, as I could not condescend to be patronized in this way. Depressed

in hope, but strengthened in will, I did not deliver
any more of my letters, since they were all to
physicians, and I could not hope to be more successful in other quarters. I went home, therefore,
determined to commence practice as a stranger.

The result of my experiment discouraged my
sister greatly. After meditating for some time,
she suddenly said, "Marie, I read in the paper
this morning of a dressmaker who wanted some
one to sew for her. I know how to sew well: I
shall go there, and you can attend to our little
household. No one here knows me, and I do not
think there is any thing wrong in my trying to earn
some money."

She was determined, and went. I put up my
sign, and spent my time in attending to the household duties, and in reading in order to gain information of the country and the people. Occa-
sionally I took walks through different parts of the
city, to learn, from the houses and their surroundings, the character of life in New York. I am
sure that though, perhaps, I appeared idle, I was
not so in reality; for during this time I learned the
philosophy of American life.

But our stock of money was becoming less and less.
To furnish the rooms had cost us comparatively

little, as we had brought a complete set of household furniture with us; but paying the rent and completing the arrangements had not left us more than enough to live upon, in the most economical manner, until the 1st of August. My sister obtained the place at the dressmaker's; and after working a week from seven in the morning until twelve (when she came home to dinner), then from one in the afternoon until seven in the evening, she received two dollars and seventy-five cents as the best sewer of six. She brought home the hardly earned money with tears in her eyes; for she had expected at least three dollars for the week's work. She had made each day a whole muslin dress, with the trimmings. And this was not all: the dressmaker often did not pay on Saturday nights, because, as she said, people did not pay her punctually; and the poor girls received their wages by six or eight shillings at a time. For the last two weeks of my sister's work, she received her payment seven weeks after she had left.

We lived in this manner until the middle of July, when I lost patience; for practice did not come as readily as I wished, nor was I in a position for making money in any other way. My sister, usually so cheerful and happy, grew grave from the unusual work and close confinement. One of these nights, on lying down to sleep, she burst into tears, and told me of her doubts and fears for the future. I soothed her as well as I could, and she fell asleep. For myself, I could not sleep, but lay awake all night meditating what I could possibly do. Should I write home, requesting help from my father? He certainly would have given it; for we had received a letter two weeks before, offering us all desirable aid. No: all my pride rebelled against it. "I must help myself," I thought, "and that to-morrow."

The next morning, my sister left me as usual. I went out, and walked through the city to Broadway; turning into Canal Street, where I had formed an acquaintance with a very friendly German woman by purchasing little articles at various times at her store. I entered without any particular design, and exchanged a few commonplaces with her about the weather. Her husband stood talking with a man about worsted goods, and their conversation caught my ear. The merchant was complaining because the manufacturer did not supply him fast enough: upon which the man answered, that it was very difficult to get good hands to work; and that, besides, he had more orders than it was possible to fill; naming several merchants whose names I had seen in Broadway, who were also complaining because he did not supply them. After he had left, I asked carelessly what kind of articles were in demand, and was shown a great variety of worsted fancy-goods. A thought entered my brain. I left the store, and, walking down Broadway, asked at one of the stores that had been mentioned for a certain article of worsted goods, in order to learn the price. Finding this enormous, I did not buy it; and returned home, calculating on my way how much it would cost to manufacture these articles, and how much profit could be made in making them on a large scale. I found that two hundred per cent profit might be made by going to work in the right way. My sister came home, as usual, to dinner. I sat down with her, but could not eat. She looked at me anxiously, and said, " I hope you are not sick again. Oh, dear! what shall we do if you get sick?" I had been ill for a week, and she feared a relapse. I said nothing of my plan, but consoled her in respect to my health.

As soon as she had left, I counted my money. But five dollars remained. If I had been dependent upon money for cheerfulness, I should certainly have been discouraged. I went to John Street, and, entering a large worsted store, inquired of a cheerful-looking girl the wholesale price of the best Berlin wool; how many colors could be had in a pound; &c. The pleasant and ready answers that I received in my native tongue induced me to tell her frankly that I wanted but a small quantity at that time, but that I intended to make an experiment in manufacturing worsted articles; and, if successful, would like to open a small credit, which she said they generally would do when security was given.

I purchased four and a half dollars' worth of worsted; so that fifty cents were left in my pocket when I quitted the store. I then went to the office of a German newspaper, where I paid twenty-five cents for advertising for girls who understood all kinds of knitting. When my sister came home at night, the worsted was all sorted on the table in parcels for the girls who would come the next morning, while I was busily engaged in the experiment of making little worsted tassels. I had never been skilful in knitting; but in this I succeeded so well, that I could have made a hundred yards of tassels in one day. My sister turned pale on seeing all this; and hurriedly asked, "How much money have you spent?" — "All, my dear Anna," answered I; "all, except twenty-five cents, which will be sufficient to buy a pound of beefsteak and potatoes for to-morrow's dinner. Bread, tea, and sugar we have still in the house; and to-morrow night you will bring home your twenty-two shillings." "May you succeed, Marie! that is all I have to say," was her reply. She learned of me that evening how to make the tassels; and we worked till midnight, finishing a large number.

The next day was Saturday, and some women really came to get work. I gave them just enough for one day, keeping one day's work in reserve. The day was spent busily in arranging matters, so that, on Monday morning, I might be able to carry a sample of the manufactured articles to those stores that I had heard mentioned as not being sufficiently supplied.

In the evening, my sister came home without her money: the dressmaker had gone into the country in the afternoon, without paying the girls. She was more than sad, and I felt a little uncomfortable; for what was I to do, without money to provide for the next two days, or to pay those girls on Monday with whose work I might not be satisfied? What was to be done? To go down to our landlord, the grocer, and ask him to advance us a few dollars? No: he was a stranger, and had no means of knowing that we would return the money. Besides, I did not wish the people in the house to know our condition.

My resolution was taken. I proposed to my sister to go to the market with me to buy meat and fruit for the morrow. She looked at me with blank astonishment; but, without heeding it, I said calmly, taking from the bureau-drawer the chain of my watch, "Anna, opposite the market, there is a pawnbroker. No one knows us; and, by giving a fictitious name, we can get money, without thanking any one for it." She was satisfied; and, taking a little basket, we went on our errand. I asked of the pawnbroker six dollars, under the name of Müller, and received the money; after which we made our purchases, and went home in quite good spirits.

On Monday morning, the knitters brought home their work. I paid them, and gave them enough for another day; after which I set about finishing each piece, completing the task about two in the afternoon. This done, I carried the articles to Broadway; and, leaving a sample in a number of stores, received orders from them for several dozens.* I then went to the worsted store in John Street, where I also obtained orders for the manufactured articles, together with ten dollars' worth of worsted on credit; having first given my name and residence to the book-keeper, with the names of the stores from which I had received orders. In the evening, when my sister came home, I was, therefore, safely launched into a manufacturing business. The news cheered her greatly; but she could not be induced to quit her sewing. The new business had sprung up so rapidly and pleasantly, that she could not trust in the reality of its existence.

I must tell you here something of the social life that we led. We had brought a number of friendly letters with us from our acquaintances in Berlin to their friends and relatives in America; all of which, upon our arrival, we sent by post, with the exception of two, — the one sent by a neighbor to his son, Albert C.; the other to a young artist; both of whom called for their letters. About four weeks

---

* Here I have to remark, that, not being able to speak English, I conducted my business at the different stores either in German or French, as I easily found some of the *employées* who could speak one of these languages.

after we .were settled in New York, we received a
call from some young men whose sisters had been
schoolmates of my sisters in Berlin, who came to
inquire of us where to find Mr. C. We could give
them no information, as we had not seen him since
he called for his letter ; neither did we now see any
thing of the G.'s : but the acquaintance thus formed
with these young men was continued, and our soli-
tude was now and then enlivened by an hour's call
from them.   Soon after I had commenced my new
business, they came one day in company with Mr.
C., whom they had met accidently in the street,
and, on his expressing a wish to see us, had taken
the liberty to bring to our house.

My business continued to prosper ; and, by constantly offering none but the best quality of goods
for sale, in a very short time I had so much to do,
that my whole time in the day was occupied with
out-door business, and I was forced to sit up at
night with my sister to prepare work for the knitters.   At one time, we had constantly thirty girls
in our employ ; and in this way I became acquainted with many of those unfortunates who had been
misled and ruined on their arrival by persons pre-
tending friendship.   Two of these in particular
interested me greatly.   One, the grand-daughter

of Krummacher, and bearing his name, was the daughter of a physician, who had come to this country, hoping to find a place as governess. Poor girl! she was a mere wreck when I found her, and all my efforts to raise her up were in vain. She was sick, and in a terrible mental condition. We took her into our house, nursed her and cared for her, and, when she had recovered, supplied her with work; for which we paid her so well, that she always had three dollars a week, which paid for her board and washing. It was twice as much as she could earn, yet not enough to make her feel reconciled with life. At one time, she did not come to us for a whole week. I went to see her, and her landlady told me that she was melancholy. I persuaded her to come and stay with us for a few days; but, in spite of all my friendly encouragement, I could not succeed in restoring her to cheerfulness. She owned that she could not work merely to live: she did not feel the pangs of hunger; but she felt the want of comforts to which she had been accustomed, and which, in our days, are regarded as necessities. She attempted to find a situation as governess; but her proficiency in music, French, and drawing, counted as nothing. She had no city references; and, having been two years in

New York, dared not name the place to which she
had been conducted on her arrival.   She left us at
last in despair, after having been a week with us.
She never called again, and I could not learn from
her landlady where she had gone.   Three months
afterwards, I heard from one of the girls in our
employ that she had married a poor shoemaker in
order to have a home ; but I never learned whether
this was true.   About a year later, I met her in
the Bowery, poorly but cleanly dressed.   She
hastily turned away her face on seeing me ; and I
only caught a glimpse of the crimson flush that
overspread her countenance.

The other girl that I referred to was a Miss
Mary ——, who came with her mother to this
country, expecting to live with a brother.   They
found the brother married, and unwilling to support his sister ; while his wife was by no means
friendly in her reception of his mother.   The good
girl determined to earn a support for her mother,
and a pretended friend offered to take care of their
things until she could find work and rent lodgings.
After four weeks' search, she found a little room
and bedroom in a rear-building in Elizabeth Street,
at five dollars a month ; and was preparing to move,
when her *friend* presented a bill of forty dollars for

his services. She could only satisfy his. rapacity
by selling every thing that she could possibly spare :
after which she commenced to work ; and as she
embroidered a great deal, besides working for me
(for which I paid her six dollars a week), for a time
she lived tolerably well. After some time, her mo
ther fell ill ; and she had to nurse her and attend to
the household, as well as labor for their support.
It was a trying time for the poor girl. She sought
her brother ; but he had moved to the West. I
did all that I could for her ; but this was not half
enough : and, after I had quitted the manufacturing
business and left the city, my sister heard that she
had drowned herself in the Hudson, because her
mother's corpse was lying in the house, while she
had not a cent to give it burial, or to buy a piece
of bread, without selling herself to vice.

Are not these two terrible romances of New-
York life ? And many besides did I learn among
these poor women ; so many, indeed, that I forget
the details of all. Stories of this kind are said to
be without foundation : I say that there are more
of them in our midst than it is possible to imagine.
Women of good education, but without money, are
forced to earn their living. They determine to
leave their home, either because false pride pre-

vents their seeking work where they have been
brought up as *ladies*, or because this work is so
scarce that they cannot earn by it even a life of
semi-starvation; while they are encouraged to believe that in this country they will readily find
proper employment. They are too well educated
to become domestics; better educated, indeed,
than are half the teachers here: but modesty,
and the habit of thinking that they must pass
through the same legal ordeal as in Europe, prevent them from seeking places in this capacity.
They all know how to embroider in the most beautiful manner; and, knowing that this is well paid
for in Europe, seek to find employment of this kind
in the stores. Not being able to speak English,
they believe the stories of the clerks and proprie-
tors, and are made to work at low wages, and are
often swindled out of their money. They feel home-
sick, forlorn and forsaken in the world. Their
health at length fails them, and they cannot earn
bread enough to keep themselves from starvation.
They are too proud to beg; and the consequence is,
that they walk the streets, or throw themselves into
the river.

I met scores of these friendless women. Some
I took into my house; for others I found work,

and made myself a sort of guardian ; while to others I gave friendship to keep them morally alive. It is a curious fact, that these women are chiefly Germans. The Irish resort at once to beggary, or are inveigled into brothels, as soon as they arrive ; while the French are always intriguing enough either to put on a white cap and find a place as *bonne,* or to secure a *private* lover.

. I am often in despair about the helplessness of women, and the readiness of men to let them earn money in abundance by shame, while they grind them down to the merest pittance for honorable work. Shame on society, that women are forced to surrender themselves to an abandoned life and death, when so many are enjoying wealth and luxury in extravagance ! I do not wish them to divide their estates with the poor ; I am no friend to communism in any form : I only wish institutions that shall give to women an education from childhood, that will enable them, like young men, to earn their livelihood. These weak women are the last to come forth to aid in their emancipation from inefficient education. We cannot calculate upon these : we must educate the children for better positions, and leave the adults to their destiny.

How many women marry only for a shelter or a

home! How often have I been the confidante of girls, who the day before, arrayed in satin, had given their hands to rich men before the altar, while their hearts were breaking with suppressed agony! and this, too, among Americans, this great, free nation, who, notwithstanding, let their women starve. It is but lately that a young woman said to me, " I thank Heaven, my dear doctor, that you are a woman; for now I can tell you the truth about my health. It is not my body that is sick, but my heart. These flounces and velvets cover a body that is sold, — sold legally to a man who could pay my father's debts." Oh! I scorn men, sometimes, from the bottom of my heart. Still this is wrong: for it is the women's, the mothers' fault, in educating their daughters to be merely beautiful machines, fit to ornament a fine establishment; while, if they do not succeed in gaining this, there is nothing left but wretchedness of mind and body. Women, there is a connection between the Fifth Avenue and the Five Points! Both the rich and the wretched are types of womanhood; both are linked together, forming one great body; and both have the same part in good and evil. I can hardly leave this subject, though it may seem to have little to do with my American experience; but a word spoken from a full heart not only gives relief, but may fall on *one* listening ear, and take root there.

I must now return to my new enterprise. The business paid well: and, although I was often forced to work with my sister till the dawn of morning, we were happy; for we had all that we needed, and I could write home that the offered assistance was superfluous. Here I must say, that I had resolved, on leaving Berlin, never to ask for aid, in order that I might be able with perfect freedom to carry out my plans independently of my family. How this was ever to be done, I did not yet see; though I had a good opportunity to learn, from life and from the papers, what I had to expect here. But this mode of instruction, though useful to one seeking to become a philosopher, was very unsatisfactory to me. The chief thing that I learned was, that I must acquire English before I could undertake any thing. And this was the most difficult point to overcome. I am not a linguist by nature: all that I learn of languages must be obtained by the greatest perseverance and industry; and, for this, my business would not allow me time.

Shortly after I had fairly established myself in the manufacturing business, I received news from

Berlin, that Sister Catherine had left the Hospital
Charité, and was intending to join me in America,
in order to aid me in carrying out my plan for the
establishment of a hospital for women in the New
World. The parties interested in her had finally
succeeded in placing her in the wished-for position,
thus disconnecting her from the sisterhood. But,
after my departure, the position became greatly mo-
dified in rank, and inferior in character. Private
reasons besides made it disagreeable for her to remain there any longer; and in this moment she
remembered my friendship towards her, and in
the unfortunate belief that she shared with many
others, that all that I designed to do I could do at
once, resolved to come to me, and offer her assistance. She joined us on the 22d of August, and
was not a little disappointed to find me in the tassel
instead of the medical line. The astonishment
with which her acquaintances in Berlin heard her
announce her intention of going to seek help from
a person to whom she had been less than a friend,
could not be expressed in words; and she told me
that the annoyance that they manifested was really
the chief stimulus that decided her to come at last.
She arrived without a cent. Having always found
friends enough ready to supply her with money,

whenever she wished to establish a temporary hospital, it had never occurred to her that she should need
any for private use, beyond just enough to furnish the
simple blue merino dress of the sisterhood, which
had often been provided for her by the Kaiserswerth
Institute. But here she was; and she very soon
learned to understand the difficulties which must
be overcome before I could enter again into my
profession. She became satisfied, and lived with
us, sharing equally in whatever we had ourselves.
There is a peculiar satisfaction in showing kindness
to a person who has injured us, though unconsciously, under different circumstances: and, in her
case, she was not entirely unconscious of the harm
she had done me; for she confessed to me while in
America, that her acquaintance was courted by all
those who had been thwarted in their opposition
by my appointment, and that she knew well that
they sought every opportunity to annoy me.

On the 18th of September, a sister, one year
younger than myself, joined us; having been
tempted by our favorable accounts to try a life of
adventure. We were now four in the family. But
Catherine gradually grew discontented. Having
been accustomed to the comforts afforded in large
institutions, and to receiving attentions from the

most aristocratic families of Prussia, the monotonous life that we led was only endurable to her so long as the novelty lasted. This soon wore off, and she became anxious for a change. She had heard her fellow-passengers speak of a Pastor S., who had been sent to America as a missionary; and she begged me to seek him out, and take her to him, that she might consult him as to what she had best do. I did so, and she soon became acquainted with his family. Mr. S. exerted himself in her behalf, and secured her a place as nurse in the Home for the Friendless, where she had the charge of some thirty children. This was a heavy task; for, though none were under a year old, she was constantly disturbed through the night, and could get but a few hours' consecutive sleep. Besides, she could not become reconciled to washing under the hydrant in the morning, and to being forced to mingle with the commonest Irish girls. She was in every respect a lady, and had been accustomed to have a servant at her command, even in the midst of the typhus-fever in the desolate districts of Silesia; while here she was not even treated with humanity. This soon grew unbearable; and she returned to us on the 16th of October, after having been only ten days in the institution.

So eager was she to make her escape, that she did
not even ask for the two dollars that were due her
for wages. But we could not receive her; for we
had taken another woman in her place, as friendless and as penniless as she. Besides, a misfortune
had just fallen upon us. During the night before,
our doors had been unlocked, our bureau-drawers
inspected, and all our money, amounting to fifty-two
dollars, carried off; and, when Catherine arrived,
we were so poor that we had to borrow the bread
and milk for our breakfast. Fortunately, the day
before, I had refused the payment due me for a
large bill of goods; and this came now in a very
good time. I did not feel justified, however, in
increasing the family to five after our loss; nor did
she claim our assistance, but went again to Pastor
S., who had invited her to visit his family. With
his assistance, she obtained some private nursing,
which maintained her until the congregation had
collected money enough to enable her to return to
Berlin; which she did on the 2d of December.
Having many friends in the best circles of that city,
she immediately found a good practice again; and is
now, as she says, enjoying life in a civilized manner.

We moved at once from the scene of the rob-
bery, and took a part of a house in Monroe Street,

for which we paid two hundred dollars a year. Our business continued good, and I had some prospects of getting into practice. But, with spring, the demand for worsted goods ceased; and as my practice brought me work, but no money, I was forced to look out for something else to do. By accident, I saw in a store a coiffure made of silk, in imitation of hair, which I bought; but I found, on examination, that I could not manufacture it, as it was machine-work. I went, therefore, to Mr. G., and proposed to establish a business with him, in which he should manufacture these coiffures, while I would sell them by wholesale to the merchants with whom I was acquainted. Mr. G. had completely ruined himself during the winter by neglecting his business and meddling with Tammany-Hall politics, which had wasted his money and his time. He had not a single workman in his shop when I called, and was too much discouraged to think of any new enterprise; but, on my telling him that I would be responsible for the first outlay, he engaged hands, and, in less than a month, had forty-eight persons busily employed. In this way I earned money during the spring, and freed myself from the obligations, which his kindness in receiving us the spring before had laid upon us.

My chief business now was to sell the goods manufactured by Mr. G. Our worsted business was very small; and the prospect was that it would cease entirely, and that the coiffure that we made would not long continue in fashion. Some other business, therefore, had to be found, especially as it was impossible for us to lay up money. Our family now consisted of myself and two sisters, the friend that was staying with us, and a brother, nineteen years of age, who had joined us during the winter, and who, though an engineer and in good business, was, like most young men, thought-less, and more likely to increase than to lighten our burdens. Our friend Mr. C., who had be-come our constant visitor, planned at this time a journey to Europe; so that our social life seemed also about to come to an end.

On the 13th of May, 1854, as I was riding down to the stores on my usual business, reveries of the past took possession of my mind. Almost a year in America, and not one step advanced towards my purpose in coming hither! It was true that I had a comfortable home, with enough to live upon, and had repaid my sister the money that I had borrowed from her on our arrival; yet what kind of a life was it that I was leading, in a business

foreign to my nature and inclinations, and without
even the prospect of enlarging this? These re-
flections made me so sad, that, when I reached the
store, the book-keeper noticed my dejection, and
told me, by way of cheering me, that he had another
order for a hundred dollars' worth of goods, &c.;
but this did not relieve me. I entered the omnibus
again, speculating constantly on what I should do
next; when a thought suddenly dawned upon me.
Might not the people in the Home for the Friendless be able to give me advice? I had hardly
conceived the idea, when I determined to ride
directly up there, instead of stopping at the street
in which I lived. I thought, besides, that some
employment might be found for my sister Anna, in
which she could learn the English language, for
which she had evinced some talent, while I had
decided that I could never become master of it. I
had seen the matron, Miss Goodrich, once when
I called there on Catherine S. She had a humane
face, and I was persuaded that I should find a
friend in her. I was not mistaken. I told her of
my plans in coming here, and of our present mode
of·life and prospects; and confided to her my disappointment and dejection, as well as my determination to persevere courageously. She seemed to

understand and to enter into my feelings, and
promised to see Dr. Elizabeth Blackwell, whom
she advised me to call upon at once.

I went home full of the hope and inspiration of
a new life. Dear Mary, you can hardly comprehend the happiness of that morning. I was not
suffering, it is true, for the necessaries of life; but,
what was far worse, I suffered from the feeling
that I lived for no purpose but to eat and to drink.
I had no friends who were interested in the pursuits
towards which my nature inclined; and I saw
crowds of arrogant people about me, to whom I
could not prove that I was their equal in spite of
their money. My sisters had not seen me so cheerful since our arrival in America, and thought that
I had surely discovered the philosopher's stone. I
told them of what I had done, and received their
approbation.

On the morning of the 15th of May, — the anni-
versary of the death of Dr. Schmidt and of my
greatest joy and my greatest misery, — we received
a call from Miss Goodrich, who told us that she
had seen Dr. Elizabeth Blackwell, and thought that
she had also procured a suitable place for my sister.
She gave us the addresses of Dr. Blackwell and of
Miss Catherine Sedgwick. We called first upon the

9

latter, who was extremely kind ; and although she had quite misunderstood our wishes, — having exerted herself to procure a place for my sister in a way that manifested the belief that we had neither a home nor the means to live, — yet her friendliness and readiness to assist us made us for ever grateful to her. At that time we did not know her standing in society, and looked upon her merely as a benevolent and wealthy woman. We soon learned more of her, however: for, though unsuccessful in her first efforts, she shortly after sent for my sister, having secured her a place in Mr. Theodore Sedgwick's family; which was acceptable, inasmuch as it placed her above the level of the servants. She remained there seven weeks, and then returned home.

On the same morning, I saw Dr. Elizabeth Blackwell ; and from this call of the 15th of May I date my new life in America. She spoke a little German, and understood me perfectly when I talked. I gave her all my certificates for inspection, but said nothing to her of my plans in coming to America. It would have seemed too ludicrous for me in my position to tell her that I entertained the idea of interesting the people in the establishment of a hospital for women. I hardly know

what I told her, indeed; for I had no other plan of
which to speak, and therefore talked confusedly,
like an adventurer. I only know that I said that
I would take the position of nurse, if I could enter
one of the large hospitals, in order to learn the
manner in which they were managed in this country.

I cannot comprehend how Dr. Blackwell could
ever have taken so deep an interest in me as she
manifested that morning; for I never in my life
was so little myself. Yet she did take this interest;
for she gave me a sketch of her own experience in
acquiring a medical education, and explained the
requirements for such in this country, and the obstacles that are thrown in the way of women who
seek to become physicians. She told me of her plan
of founding a hospital, — the long-cherished idea
of my life; and said that she had opened a little
dispensary — the charter for which was procured
during the preceding winter, under the name of
"The New-York Infirmary for Indigent Women
and Children" — on the 1st of May, two weeks
before, and which was designed to be the nucleus
for this hospital, where she invited me to come and
assist her. She insisted that, first of all, I should
learn English; and offered to give me lessons twice

a week, and also to make efforts to enable me to
enter a college to acquire the title of M.D., which
I had not the right to attach to my name. I left
her after several hours' conversation, and we parted
friends.

I continued my work at home ; going regularly to
Dr. Blackwell to receive lessons in English, and
to assist her in the dispensary. As we grew better
acquainted, I disclosed more to her of the fact, that
I had a fixed plan in coming to this country; which
increased her interest in me. She wrote in my
behalf to the different colleges, and at length succeeded in obtaining admission for me to the
Cleveland Medical College (Western Reserve) on
the most favorable terms ; credit being given me
on the lecture-fees for an indefinite time.

Here I must stop to tell you why this credit was
necessary. The articles that I had manufactured
had gone out of fashion in May: and I could not
invent any thing new, partly because I no longer
felt the same interest as before, knowing that I
should soon go to a medical college ; and partly
because the articles then in fashion were cheaper
when imported. We had to live for a little while
on the money that we had laid up, until I procured
a commission for embroidering caps. It is per-

fectly wonderful into what kinds of business I was
forced, all foreign to my taste.

And here let me tell you some secrets of this
kind of business, in which hundreds of women
starve, and hundreds more go down to a life of
infamy. Cap-making (the great business of Water
Street of New York) gives employment to thousands of unfortunates. For embroidering caps,
the wholesale dealer pays seven cents each; and
for making up, three cents. To make a dozen a
day, one must work for sixteen hours. The embroidering is done in this wise: I received the
cut cloth from the wholesale dealer; drew the pat-
tern upon each cap; gave them, with three cents'
worth of silk, to the embroiderer, who received three
cents for her work; then pressed and returned
them; thus making one cent on each for myself.
By working steadily for sixteen hours, a girl could
embroider fifteen in a day. I gave out about six
dozen daily; earning, like the rest, fifty cents a day:
unless I chose to do the stamping and pressing at
night, and to embroider a dozen during the day; in
which case, I earned a dollar.

One can live in this way for a little while, until
health fails, or the merchant says that the work
has come to an end. You will think this terrible

again. Oh, no! this is not terrible. The good men
provide in another way. They tell every woman of
a prepossessing appearance, that it is wrong in her
to work so hard; that many a man would be glad
to care for her; and that many women live quite
comfortably with the help of *a friend*. They say,
further, that it is lonely to live without ever going
to church, to the concert and theatre; and that if
these women would only permit the speakers to
visit them, and to attend them to any of these places,
they would soon find that they would no longer be
obliged to work so hard. This is the polished talk
of gentlemen who enjoy the reputation of piety and
respectability, and who think it a bad speculation
to pay women liberally for their work. So it would
be, in truth; for these poor creatures would not be
so willing to abandon themselves to a disreputa-
ble life, if they could procure bread in any other
way.

During the summer of 1854, I took work on
commission from men of this sort. While in Berlin, I had learned from the prostitutes in the hospital in what manner educated women often became
what they then were. The average story was always the same. The purest love made them weak;
their lover deceived and deserted them; their

family cast them off by way of punishment. In their disgrace, they went to bury themselves in large cities, where the work that they could find scarcely gave them their daily bread. Their employers, attracted by their personal appearance and the refinement of their speech and manners, offered them assistance in another way, in which they could earn money without work. In despair, they accepted the proposals ; and sunk gradually, step by step, to the depths of degradation, as depicted by Hogarth in the " Harlot's Progress." In New York, I was thrown continually among men who were of the stamp that I described before ; and can say, even from my own experience, that no man is ever more polite, more friendly, or more kind, than one who has impure wishes in his heart. It is really so dangerous for a woman of refined nature to go to such stores, that I never suffered my sister to visit them ; not because I feared that she would listen to these men, but because I could not endure the thought that so innocent and beautiful a girl should come in contact with them, or even breathe the same atmosphere. When fathers are unwilling that their daughters shall enter life as physicians, lawyers, merchants, or in any other public capacity, it is simply because they belong to the class that so

contaminates the air, that none can breathe it but
themselves; or because, from being thrown constantly in contact with such men, they arrive at the
same point at which I then stood, and say to themselves, "*I* can afford to meet such men.   I am
steeled by my knowledge of mankind, and supported
by the philosophy that I have learned during years
of trial.   It cannot hurt *me*; but, by all means,
spare the young and beautiful the same experience!"

I dealt somewhat haughtily with the merchants
whom I have described, in a manner that at once
convinced them of my position.   But the consequence was, that the embroidery commission, which
had commenced so favorably, suddenly ceased,
"*because the Southern trade had failed:*" in truth,
because I would not allow any of these men to say
any more to me than was absolutely necessary in
our business.   My income became less and less,
and we were forced to live upon the money that
we had laid up during the year.   I did not look for
any new sources of employment, for I was intending to go to Cleveland in October; while my next
sister had business of her own, and Anna was engaged to be married to our friend Mr. C.   My
brother was also with them; and my mother's

brother, whom she had adopted as a child, was on his way to America.

After having settled our affairs, fifty dollars remained as my share; and, with this sum, I set out for Cleveland on the 16th of October, 1854. Dr. Elizabeth Blackwell had supplied me with the necessary medical text-books; so that I had no other expenses than my journey and the matriculation fees, which together amounted to twenty dollars, leaving thirty dollars in my possession.

I do not believe that many begin the study of medicine with so light a purse and so heavy a heart as did I. My heart was heavy for the reason that I did not know a single sentence of English. All of my study with Dr. Blackwell had been like rain-drops falling upon stone : I had profited nothing. The lectures I did not care for, since there was more need of my studying English than medicine : but the subjects were well known to me ; and I therefore reasoned, that, by hearing familiar things treated of in English, I must learn the language ; and the logic held good.

I have already told you that the Faculty had agreed to give me credit for my lecture-fees. Dr. Blackwell had written also to a lady there, who had called upon her some time before in the capacity of President of a Physiological Society, which, among other good things, had established a small fund for the assistance of women desirous of studying medicine. This lady (Mrs. Caroline M. Severance) replied in the most friendly manner, saying that I might come directly to her house, and that she would see that my board for the winter was secured by the Physiological Society over which she presided.

The journey to Cleveland was a silent but a pleasant one. Through a mishap, I arrived on Saturday night, instead of in the morning; and, being unwilling to disturb Mrs. Severance at so late an hour, went first to a hotel. But what trials I had there! No one could understand me; until at last I wrote on a slate my own name and Mrs. Severance's, with the words, "A carriage," and "To-morrow." From this the people inferred that I wished to stay at the hotel all night, and to have a carriage to take me to Mrs. Severance's the next day; as was the case. A waiter took my carpet-bag, and conducted me to a room. I could not understand his directions to the supper-room, neither could I make him understand that I wanted some supper in my own room; and the consequence was, that I went to bed hungry, having eaten nothing all day but a little bread, and an apple for luncheon.

As soon as I was dressed the next morning, I rang the bell furiously; and, on the appearance of the waiter, exclaimed, "Beefsteak!" This time he comprehended me, and went laughingly away to bring me a good breakfast. I often saw the same waiter afterwards at the hotel; and he never saw me without laughing, and exclaiming, "Beefsteak!"

In the course of the forenoon, I was taken in a carriage to the house of Mrs. Severance; but the family were not at home. I returned to the hotel, somewhat disheartened and disappointed. Although I should have supposed that death was not far off if no disappointment had happened to me when I least expected it, yet this persistent going wrong of every thing in Cleveland was really rather dispiriting. But a bright star soon broke through the clouds, in the shape of Mr. Severance, who came into the parlor directly after dinner, calling for me in so easy and so cordial a manner, that I forgot every thing, and was perfectly happy. This feeling, however, lasted only until I reached the house. I found four fine children, all full of childish curiosity to hear me talk; who, as soon as

they found that I could not make myself understood by them, looked on me with that sort of contempt peculiar to children when they discover that
a person cannot do as much as they can themselves.
Mr. Severance, too, was expecting to find me accomplished in music, " like all Germans ; " and had
to learn that I had neither voice nor ear for the art.
Mrs. Severance understood a little German, yet not
half enough to gain any idea of how much or how
little I was capable of doing ; and therefore looked
upon me with a sort of uncertainty as to what was
my real capacity. This position was more provoking than painful ; there was even something ludicrous in it : and, when not annoyed, I often went
into my room to indulge in a hearty laugh by
myself.

I met with a most cordial reception in the college. The dean (Dr. John J. Delamater) received
me like a father ; and, on the first day, I felt perfectly at home. All was going on well. I had a
home at Mrs. Severance's ; while, despite my muti-
lated English, I found many friends in the college,
when circumstances changed every thing. Some
changes occurred in Mr. Severance's business ; and
he was forced, in consequence, to give up housekeeping. At that time, I did not know that the

Physiological Society was ready to lend me money; and was therefore in great distress. I never experienced so bitter a day as that on which Mrs. Severance told me that I could stay with her no longer. It was but five weeks after my arrival, and I was not able to make myself understood in the English language, which was like chaos to me. On the same day, I well remember, that, for the first time in my life, I made an unsuccessful attempt to borrow money; and, because it was the first and the last time, it was the more painful to me to be refused. I envied the dog that lived, and was happy without troubling his brain; I envied the kitchen-maid, that did her work mechanically, and enjoyed life far more than those fitted by nature for something higher, while the world would go on just as well without them as with them.

Mrs. Severance secured a boarding-place for me for the rest of the winter; and paid my board, amounting to thirty-three dollars, from the funds of the society. I lived quietly by myself; studied six hours daily at home, with four dictionaries by me; attending six lectures a day, and going in the evening for three hours to the dissecting-rooms. I never conversed with any one in the boarding-house, nor even asked for any thing at the table;

but was supplied like a mute. This silence was
fruitful to me. About New Year, I ventured to
make my English audible; when, lo! every one understood me perfectly. From this time forward,
I sought to make acquaintances, to the especial delight of good old Dr. Delamater, who had firmly
believed that I was committing gradual suicide.
Through Mrs. Severance, I became acquainted
with Dr. Harriot K. Hunt, who was then on a
visit to Cleveland; and, through her, with the Rev.
A. D. Mayo, who was pastor of a small society
there, known as that of the Liberal Christians.

I found many dear and valued friends during my
residence in Cleveland, but none to whom I am
bound in lasting gratitude as to Mr. Mayo, who
offered me his assistance when he learned that I
was in need; my extra expenses having swallowed
up the little money that I had brought with me, so
that I had not even enough to return to my sisters
in New York. As the minister of a small congregation, advocating Liberal ideas, he had a hard
position in Cleveland, both socially and pecuniarily;
yet he offered to share his little with me. I was
forced to accept it; and I am now, and have always
been, glad that I did so. No one, that has not had
the experience, can appreciate the happiness that

comes with the feeling, that a rich man has not
cast a fragment of his superfluity towards you (and
here let me remark, that it is next to impossible to
find wealth and generosity go together in friendship), but that the help comes from one who must
work for it as well as the recipient. It proves the
existence of the mutual appreciation that is known
by the name of " friendship." The apple given by a
friend is worth ten times more than a whole orchard
bestowed in such a way as to make you feel that
the gift is but the superfluity of the donor.

I remained for ten months a member of Mr.
Mayo's family; when he received a call to Albany,
and changes had to be made in his household.
During this time, I earned a little money by giving
lessons in German, that served to cover my most
necessary expenses. For the last five months that
I spent in Cleveland, I carried in my purse one
solitary cent as a sort of talisman; firmly believing
that some day it would turn into gold: but this
did not happen; and on the day that I was expecting the receipt of the last eighteen dollars for my
lessons, which were designed to bear my expenses
to New York, I gave it to a poor woman in the
street who begged me for a cent; and it doubtless,
ere long, found its way into a gin-shop.

The twenty months that I spent in Cleveland were chiefly devoted to the study of medicine in the English language; and in this I was assisted by most noble-hearted men. Dr. Delamater's office became a pleasant spot, and its occupants a necessity to me; and, on the days that I did not meet them, my spirits fell below zero. In spite of the pecuniary distress from which I constantly suffered, I was happier in Cleveland than ever before or since. I lived in my element; having a fixed purpose in view, and enjoying the warmest tokens of real friendship. I was liked in the college; and, though the students often found it impossible to repress a hearty laugh at my ridiculous blunders in English, they always showed me respect and fellowship in the highest sense of the terms. In the beginning of the first winter, I was the only woman; after the first month, another was admitted; and, during the second winter, there were three besides myself that attended the lectures and graduated in the spring. I should certainly look upon this season as the spring-time of my life, had not a sad event thrown a gloom over the whole.

In the autumn of 1854, after deciding to go to Cleveland to resume my medical studies, I wrote to my parents to tell them of my hopes and aims.

These letters were not received with the same pleasure with which they had been written. My father, who had encouraged me before my entrance upon a public career, was not only grieved by my return to my old mode of life, but greatly opposed to it, and manifested this in the strongest words in the next letter that I received from him. My mother, on the contrary, who had not been at all enthusiastic in the beginning, was rather glad to receive the news. As I had left many good friends among the physicians of Berlin, my letters were always circulated, after their arrival, by one of their number who stood high in the profession; and, though I did not receive my father's approbation, he sent me several letters from strangers who approved my conduct, and who, after hearing my letters, had sent him congratulations upon my doings in America. How he received the respect thus manifested to him, you can judge from a passage in one of his letters, which I will quote to you : —

" I am proud of you, my daughter ; yet you give me more grief than any other of my children. If you were a young man, I could not find words in which to express my satisfaction and pride in respect to your acts ; for I know that all you

accomplish you owe to yourself: but you are a
woman, a weak woman; and all that I can do for
you now is to grieve and to weep. O my daughter! return from this unhappy path. Believe me,
the temptation of living for humanity *en masse*,
magnificent as it may appear in its aim, will lead
you only to learn that all is vanity; while the in-
gratitude of the mass for whom you choose to work
will be your compensation."

Letters of this sort poured upon me; and, when
my father learned that neither his reasoning nor
his prayers could turn me from a work which I
had begun with such enthusiasm, he began to
threaten; telling me that I must not expect any
pecuniary assistance from him; that I would con-
tract debts in Cleveland which I should never be
able to pay, and which would certainly undermine
my prospects; with more of this sort. My good
father did not know that I had vowed to myself, on
my arrival in America, that I would never ask his
aid; and besides, he never imagined that I could
go for five months with a single cent in my pocket.
Oh, how small all these difficulties appeared to me,
especially at a time when I began to speak English!
I felt so rich, that I never thought money could not
be had, whenever I wanted it in good earnest.

After having been nine months in Cleveland, I received news that my mother had left Berlin with my two youngest sisters to pay us a visit, and to see what the prospects would be for my father in case she chose to remain.   Dear Mary, shall I attempt to describe to you the feeling that overpowered me on the receipt of these tidings?   If I did, you never could feel it with me : for I could not picture in words the joy that I felt at the prospect of beholding again the mother whom I loved beyond all expression, and who was my friend besides; for we really never thought of each other in our relation of mother and child, but as two who were bound together as friends in thought and in feeling.   No : I cannot give you a description of this, especially as it was mingled with the fear that I might not have the means to go to greet her in New York before another ten months were over. Day and night, night and day, she was in my mind ; and, from the time that I had a right to expect her arrival, I counted the hours from morning until noon, and from noon until night, when the telegraph office would be closed.   At length, on the 18th of September, the despatch came, — not to me, but to my friend Mr. Mayo, — bearing the words, "Tell Marie that she must calmly and quietly receive the

news that our good mother sleeps at the bottom of
the ocean, which serves as her monument and her
grave." Mary, this is the most trying passage
that I have to write in this sketch of my life; and
you must not think me weak that tears blot the
words as I write. My mother fell a victim to sea-
sickness, which brought on a violent hemorrhage,
that exhausted the sources of life. She died three
weeks before the vessel reached the port; and my
two sisters (the one seventeen and the other nine
years of age) chose rather to have her lowered on
the Banks of Newfoundland, than bring to us a
corpse instead of the living. They were right;
and the great ocean seems to me her fitting monument.

. Of course, upon the receipt of these tidings, I
could remain no longer in Cleveland, but took my
last money, and went to New York to stay for a
while with my afflicted brother and sisters. The
journey was very beneficial to me; for, without it,
I should not have been able to go through my winter's study. During my stay in New York, I often
visited Dr. Elizabeth Blackwell, and learned that
the little dispensary was closed because her practice prevented her from attending it regularly; but
that, during my absence, she had been trying to

interest some wealthy friends in the collection of money, to enable us, after my return in the spring, to commence again upon a little larger scale. To effect this, she proposed to hold a fair during the winter after my return ; and we concluded that the first meeting for this purpose should be held during my visit in New York. She succeeded in calling together a few friends at her house, who determined to form a nucleus for a Fair Association, for the purpose of raising money for the New-York Infirmary.

I made a visit of a few days to Boston, and then returned again to Cleveland. The winter passed in very much the same manner as the first, with the difference that I spoke better English, and visited many friends whom I had made during the preceding year. In the spring of 1856, I graduated. Shortly after commencement, the Dean of the College (Dr. Delamater) called upon me at the house of a friend with whom I was staying on a visit. A call from this venerable gentleman was a thing so unusual, that numberless conjectures as to what this visit might mean flitted through my brain on my way to the parlor. He received me, as usual, paternally ; wished me a thousand blessings ; and handed back to me the note for one hundred and twenty dollars, payable in two years, which I had given for the lecture-fees; telling me, that, in the meeting of the Faculty after graduating-day, it was proposed by one of the professors to return the note to me as a gift; to which those present cheerfully gave a unanimous vote, adding their wishes for my success, and appointing Dr. Delamater as their delegate to inform me of the proceedings. This was a glorious beginning, for which I am more than thankful, and for which I was especially so at that time, when I had barely money enough to return to New York, with very small prospects of getting means wherewith to commence practice. The mention of this fact might be thought indiscreet by the Faculty in Cleveland, were they still so organized as to admit women; which, I am sorry to say, is no longer the case; though they give as their reason, that women at present have their own medical colleges, and, consequently, have no longer need of theirs.

Before I quit the subject of the Cleveland College, I must mention a fact, which may serve as an argument against the belief that the sexes cannot study together without exerting an injurious effect upon each other. During the last winter of my study, there was such emulation in respect to the

graduating honors among the candidates for gradua-
tion, comprising thirty-eight male and four female
students, that all studied more closely than they
had ever done before — the men not wishing to be
excelled by the women, nor the women by the men;
and one of the professors afterwards told me, that
whereas it was usually a difficult thing to decide
upon the three best theses to be read publicly at the
commencement, since all were more or less indif-
ferently written, this year the theses were all so
good, that it was necessary, to avoid doing absolute
injustice, to select thirteen from which parts should
be read. Does not this prove that the stimulus of
the one sex upon the other would act rather favorably than otherwise upon the profession? and
would not the very best tonic that could be given
to the individual be to pique his *amour propre* by
the danger of being excelled by one of the opposite
sex? Is not this natural? and would not this be
the best and the surest reformation of humanity
and its social condition, if left free to work out its
own development?

On the day following the visit of Dr. Delamater,
I received a letter from my brother-in-law, in which
he told me that his business compelled him to go to
Europe for half a year; and that he had, therefore,

made arrangements for me to procure money, in case that I should need it to commence my practice. He said that he intended to assist me afterwards; but that, as he thought it best for my sister (his wife) to live out of New York during his absence, he was willing to lend me as much money as I required until his return. I accepted his offer with infinite pleasure; for it was another instance of real friendship. He was by no means a rich man, but was simply in the employ of a large importing house.

With these prospects I left Cleveland. Immediately after my arrival in New York, I began to look out for a suitable office; consulting Dr. Elizabeth Blackwell, with whom I had maintained a constant correspondence, in regard to location. I soon found that I could not obtain a respectable room without paying an exorbitant price. Some were afraid to let an office to a female physician, lest she might turn out a spiritual medium, clairvoyant, hydropathist, &c.; others, who believed me when I told them that I had a diploma from a regular school, and should never practise contrary to its requirements, inquired to what religious denomination I belonged, and whether I had a private fortune, or intended to support myself by my prac-

tice ; while the third class, who asked no questions
at all, demanded three dollars a day for a back
parlor alone, without the privilege of putting a
sign on the house or the door. Now, all this may
be very aggravating, when it is absolutely necessary
that one should have a place upon which to put a
sign to let the world know that she is ready to try
her skill upon suffering humanity ; but it has such a
strongly ludicrous side, that I could not be provoked,
in spite of all the fatigue and disappointment of
wandering over the city, when, with aching limbs,
I commenced the search afresh each morning, with
the same prospect of success. I finally gave up
looking for a room, and accepted Dr. Elizabeth
Blackwell's offer to occupy her back parlor (the
front one serving as her own office) ; of which I
took possession on the 17th of April.

Meanwhile, I had regularly attended the Thurs-
day fair-meetings ; wondering how persons could
afford to meet to so little purpose. There was
scarcely any life in these gatherings ; and, when I
saw ladies come week after week to resume the
knitting of a baby's stocking (which was always
laid aside again in an hour or two, without any
marked progress), I began to doubt whether the
sale of these articles would ever bring ten thousand

cents, instead of the ten thousand dollars which it
was proposed at the first meeting to raise in order
to buy a house. I used to say on Wednesday,
"To-morrow we have our fair-meeting. I wonder
whether there will be, as usual, two and a half persons present, or three and three-quarters."

I grew at length heartily sick of this kind of
effort, and set about speculating what better could
be done. The idea occurred to me to go from
house to house, and ask for a dime at each, which,
if given, would amount to ten dollars a day; and,
with the money thus collected daily for half a year,
to establish a nucleus hospital, which, as a fixed
fact, should stimulate its friends to further assistance.

I took my note-book, and wrote out the whole
plan, and also calculated the expenses of such a
miniature hospital as I proposed; including furniture, beds, household utensils; every thing, in short,
that was necessary in such an institution. With
this book, which I still have in my possession, I
went one evening into Dr. Blackwell's parlor, and,
seating myself, told her that *I* could not work any
longer for the fair in the way that the ladies were
doing; and then read my plan to her, which I advocated long and earnestly. She finally agreed with

me that it would be better speedily to establish a
small hospital than to wait for the large sum that
had been proposed; though she did not approve of
the scheme' of the dime collection, fearing that I
would not only meet with great annoyances, but
would also injure my health in the effort. At that
time, after some discussion, I agreed with her:
now I think that this plan would have been better
than that which I afterwards followed. On the
same evening, I proposed, and we agreed, that, on
a year from that day (the 1st of May, 1857), the
New-York Infirmary should be opened.

I went to rest with a light heart, but rose sor-
rowfully in the morning. "In one year from
to-day, the Infirmary must be opened," said I to
myself; "and the funds towards it are two pairs
of half-knit babies' stockings." The day was passed
in thinking what was the next best scheme to raise
money for its foundation. At length I remembered
my visit to Boston, and some friends there whose
influence might help me *to beg* for an *institution for
American women*. For myself I could never have
begged; I would sooner have drowned myself:
now I determined to beg money from Americans to
establish an institution for their own benefit. This
plan was disclosed to Dr. Blackwell, and agreed

upon, as there was nothing risked in it; I taking
the whole responsibility.

On the next day, the fair-meeting was held at
Dr. Blackwell's. The new plan was brought forward; and, although it was as yet nothing but a
plan, it acted like a warm, soft rain upon a field
after a long drought. The knitting and sewing
(for which I have a private horror under all conditions) were laid aside, to my great relief; and the
project was talked of with so much enthusiasm, that
I already saw myself in imagination making my
evening visits to the patients in the New-York Infirmary; while all the members present (and there
were unusually many; I think, six or seven) discussed the question the next day among their circles
of friends, whether Henry Ward Beecher or a physician of high standing should make the opening
speech in the institution.

This excitement increased the interest exceedingly, and the succeeding meetings were quite enthusiastic. The babies' stockings were never again
resumed (don't think that, because I detested those
stockings so much, I am cruel enough to wish the
little creatures to go barefoot); but plans were
made for raising money in New York, and for getting articles for sale on a larger scale. Dr. Black-

well wrote to her sister, Dr. Emily Blackwell, who
was at that time studying in England, requesting
her to make collections among their friends in that
country; which she did with success.

After having thus thoroughly impressed the public mind with the idea that the Infirmary must be
opened, we began to look about for a suitable
house.   In autumn, I went to Boston to see what
aid could be obtained there.   I cannot tell you
here in what manner I became acquainted with a
circle of noble women, who had both means and
the disposition to employ them for such a purpose :
it suffices to say, that I interested them in the undertaking, and obtained a hundred dollars towards
the expenses of the fair, together with a promise
of a large table of fancy-goods, and an invitation
to come again in case any further aid was needed.
At the end of three weeks, I left Boston for Philadelphia; but here I was not successful, as all who
were interested in the medical education of women
contributed largely already to the Philadelphia
College.   A small table of fancy-goods was the
result of my visit there.   The money and promise
of goods that I received in Boston stimulated our
friends in New York to such a degree, that, in spite
of Dr. Elizabeth Blackwell's doubts as to whether

we should cover the expenses, the fair realized a
thousand dollars. Yet this was not half sufficient
to commence the proposed hospital; and ·I therefore proposed to Dr. Elizabeth Blackwell that I
should go on another begging tour through New
England, while she and her sister (Dr. Emily
Blackwell, who had arrived from England a week
before the fair) should arrange matters in New
York, where they had more acquaintances than I.
I went for the second time to Boston in February,
and met with unexpected success; bringing back
about six hundred dollars in cash, with promises
of a like sum for the ensuing two years. I had
represented our scheme as a three-years' experiment. In the mean time, the Drs. Blackwell had
hired a large, old-fashioned house, No. 64, Bleeker
Street, which we had looked at together, and which
was very well suited to our purpose, devoting the
rest of their time chiefly to endeavors to interest
the Legislature in our enterprise; the result of
which was, that, though nothing was granted us
that spring, the next winter, when we could show
our institution in operation, the usual dispensary
grant was extended to us.

On the 3d of April, I returned from Boston,
and almost immediately went to work with some

of our lady-managers to order beds and to furnish the house and dispensary, and also to superintend the internal changes. After five weeks of hard work, I had the pleasure, on the 15th of May, 1857, of listening in the wards of the New-York Infirmary to the opening speeches delivered by the Rev. Henry Ward Beecher, Dr. Elder, and Rev. Dudley Tyng.

A few days afterwards, I admitted the first house-patient and opened the dispensary, which I attended two days in the week; Drs. Elizabeth and Emily Blackwell taking charge of it for the remaining four days. I had offered two years' gratuitous services as my contribution to the Infirmary, remaining there not only as resident physician, but also as superintendent of the household and general manager; and attending to my private practice during the afternoon. The institution grew rapidly, and the number of dispensary patients increased to such an extent, that the time from seven in the morning until one in the afternoon was wholly occupied in the examination of cases. In the second year of the existence of the Infirmary, the state of Dr. Elizabeth Blackwell's health compelled her to go to Europe: and for nine months Dr. Emily Blackwell and I took charge of the business, which at this time was considerable; the attendance at the dispensary averaging sixty daily.

During the course of this year, I received letters from some of the Trustees of the New-England Female Medical College in Boston, inquiring whether I were inclined to take charge of a hospital in connection with that institution. A consultation on the subject with Drs. Elizabeth and Emily Blackwell seemed to prove to us, that by doing this, and helping the college to attain its objects, we could probably best aid the cause of the medical education of women. After hesitating for a long time what course to pursue, I went to Boston in the spring of 1859, in order to define in a public address my views and position in respect to the study of medicine. I found so great a desire prevailing for the elevation of the institution to the standard of the male medical colleges, and such enthusiasm in respect to the proposed hospital, that I concluded at once to leave the Infirmary; Dr. Elizabeth Blackwell's absence having proved that it could be sustained by two, not only without loss, but with a steady increase, secured by the good done by its existence. Having fulfilled my promise of two years to the institution, on the 5th of June,

1859, I left for Boston, where I am now striving to make the hospital-department as useful as the New-York Infirmary is to the public and the students.

Now, my dear Mary, you may think me very long in my story, especially in the latter part, of which you know much already; but I could not refrain from writing fully of this part of my life, which has been the object of all my undertakings, and for which I have borne trials and overcome difficulties which would have crushed nine out of ten in my position. I do not expect that this will be the end of my usefulness; but I do expect that I shall not have to write to you any more of my doings. It was simply in order that you, my friend, should understand me fully, and because you have so often expressed a wish to know my life before we met, that I finished this work. Now you have me externally and internally, past and present: and although there have been many influences besides which have made their impressions on my peculiar development, yet they are not of a nature to be spoken of as facts; as, for instance, your friendship for me.

On looking back upon my past life, I may say that I am like a fine ship, that, launched upon high seas, is tossed about by the winds and waves, and steered against contrary currents, until finally stranded upon the shore, where, from the materials, a small boat is built, just strong enough to reach the port into which it had expected to enter with proudly swelling sails. But this ambition is entirely gone ; and I care now very little whether the people recognize what is in me or not, so long as the object for which I have lived becomes a reality.

And now, my good friend, I must add one wish before I send these last few pages to you ; namely, that I may be enabled some day to go with you to Berlin, to show you the scenes in which my childhood and youth were passed, and to teach you on the spot the difference between Europe and America. All other inducements to return have vanished. The death of my father during the last year severed the last tie that bound me to my native place. Nearly all the men who aided in promoting my wishes have passed away ; and the only stimulus that now remains to revisit the home of my youth is the wish to wander about there with you, and perhaps two or three other of my American friends. Until this can be accomplished, I hope to continue my present work in the New-England Female Medical College, which, though by no means yet

what we wish it to be, is deserving of every effort
to raise it to the stand that it ought to take among
the medical institutions of America.

Yours with love,

MARIE E. ZAKRZEWSKA.

Boston, September, 1859.

The sweet, pure song has ended. Happy she
who has been permitted to set its clear, strong notes
to music. I need not murmur that my own old
hand-organ grows useless, since it has been permitted to grind out the *key*. Yet Marie's story is
told so modestly, and with so much personal reserve,
that, for the sake of the women whom we are both
striving to help, I must be forgiven for directing
the public attention to a few of its points.

In all respects, the " little blind doctor" of the
story is the Marie Zakrzewska that we know.
The early anecdotes give us the poetic impressibility and the enduring muscular fibre, that make
themselves felt through the lively, facile nature.
The voice that ordered the fetters taken off of crazy
Jacob is the voice we still hear in the wards of the
hospital. But that poetic impressibility did not

run wild with crazy fancies when she was left to
sleep on the floor of the dead-house: the same
strong sense controlled it that started the "tassel
manufactory" in New York, where it had been
meant to open a physician's office. Only thirteen
years old when she left school, she had but little aid
beside a *steady purpose* in preparing for her career.
We hear of her slatternly habits; but who would
ever guess them, who remembers the quiet, tasteful
dress of later years?

How free from all egotism is the record! The
brain-fever which followed her attendance on her
two aunts is mentioned as quietly as if it were a
sprained foot. Who of us but can see the wearing-
away of nervous energy which took place with
the perpetual care of a cancer and a somnambulist, pressed also by the hard reading suggested
by Dr. Arthur Lütze? Berlin educated the second
La Chapelle; but it was for America, not Germany.
The dreadful tragedy of Dr. Schmidt's death is
hardly dwelt upon long enough to show its full
effects, so fearful is our friend of intruding a personal matter.

When "Woman's Right to Labor" was printed,
many persons expressed their regret that so little
was said about sin and destitution in Boston itself;

and many refused to believe that every pit-fall and
snare open in the Old World gaped as widely here.
"You have only the testimony of the girls themselves," they would reply, when I privately told
them what I had not thought it wise to print. I
have never regretted yielding to the motives which
decided me to withhold much that I knew. "If
they believe not Moses and the prophets, neither
would they believe though one rose from the dead,"
said, of old, the divine voice; and the hearts that
were not touched by what I thought it fit to tell
would never have been stirred to energy by fuller
revelations.

In these pages, authenticated by a pure and cul-
tivated woman, who holds a high position among
us, every fact at which I hinted is made plain; and
here no careless talker may challenge the record
with impunity. Here, as in New York, smooth-
faced men go on board the emigrant-ship, or the
steerage of the long-expected steamer; here, as
there, they make friendly offers and tell plausible
lies, which girls who have never walked the streets
of Berlin at night, nor seen the occupants of a hos-
pital-ward at the Charité, can hardly be expected
to estimate at their just worth. The stories which
I have told of unknown sufferers are here repeated.

The grand-daughter of Krummacher marries a poor shoemaker to save herself from vice, and poor German Mary drowns herself in the Hudson because she feels herself a burden on a heartless brother. Better far to sink beneath its waves than beneath the more remorseless flood which sweeps over all great cities. Now, when the story of the Water-street cap-makers is told, to be matched by many another in Boston itself, it is no longer some ignorant, half-trained stranger who tells the story, but the capable, skilled woman, who, educated for better things, made tassels and coiffures, and accepted commissions in embroidery, till the merchants were convinced that here, indeed, was a woman without reproach. Water-street merchants would do well to remember hereafter that the possibilities of a Zakrzewska lie hidden in every oppressed girl, and govern themselves accordingly. Think of this accomplished woman, able to earn no more than thirty-six cents a day, — a day sixteen hours long, which finished a dozen caps at three cents each! What, then, must become of clumsy and inferior work-women? Think of it long and patiently, till you come to see, as she bids you, the true relation between the idleness of women and money in the Fifth Avenue and the hunted squalor of women without money at the Five Points. Women of Boston, the parallel stands good for you. Listen, and you may hear the dull murmur of your own "Black Sea," as it surges against your gateway.

Hasten to save those whom it has not yet overwhelmed. Believe me that many of them are as pure and good as the babes whom you cradle in cambric and lace. If you will not save them, neither shall you save your own beloved ones from the current which undermines like a "back-water" your costliest churches, your most sacred homes.

CAROLINE H. DALL.

Oct. 29, 1860.

L'ENVOI.

"Unbarred be all your gates, and opened wide,
Till she who honors women shall come in !"

DANTE: Sonnet xx.

www.ingramcontent.com/pod-product-compliance
Lightning Source LLC
Chambersburg PA
CBHW020539270326
41927CB00006B/650